179916

TWAYNE'S WORLD AUTHORS SERIES

A Survey of the World's Literature

Sylvia E. Bowman, Indiana University

GENERAL EDITOR

FRANCE

Maxwell A. Smith, Guerry Professor of French, Emeritus
The University of Chattanooga
Former Visiting Professor in Modern Languages
The Florida State University

EDITOR

Chateaubriand

(TWAS 142)

TWAYNE'S WORLD AUTHORS SERIES (TWAS)

The purpose of TWAS is to survey the major writers —novelists, dramatists, historians, poets, philosophers, and critics—of the nations of the world. Among the national literatures covered are those of Australia, Canada, China, Eastern Europe, France, Germany, Greece, India, Italy, Japan, Latin America, New Zealand, Poland, Russia, Scandinavia, Spain, and the African nations, as well as Hebrew, Yiddish, and Latin Classical literatures. This survey is complemented by Twayne's United States Authors Series and English Authors Series.

The intent of each volume in these series is to present a critical-analytical study of the works of the writer; to include biographical and historical material that may be necessary for understanding, appreciation, and critical appraisal of the writer and to present all material in clear, concise English—but not to vitiate the scholarly content of the work by doing so.

Chateaubriand

By RICHARD SWITZER

California State College
San Bernardino

Twayne Publishers, Inc.   ::   New York

MANUFACTURED IN THE UNITED STATES OF AMERICA

Preface

Chateaubriand suffers, as do the foreign poets, from the undeniable fact that the necessity of translating the text in part destroys it. As with the poets, it is not merely what the author says, but the way he says it that creates his reputation. For this reason, the English-speaking student who must approach Chateaubriand through translations may indeed wonder if the author is truly worthy of the consideration he enjoys. Moreover, English and American literature lacks the long tradition of impeccable stylists so typical of France. Thus the beauties which lie in this domain may not be immediately appreciated by the reader who has not been initiated into the painstakingly analytical studies to which French literature so well lends itself.

It is easy to give to Chateaubriand only a passing glance, admitting his historical importance, but refusing to attribute to him any esthetic significance on today's literary scene. And yet, although superficially it may seem that twentieth-century literature is the antithesis of that of Chateaubriand's day, there is still a profound influence of Chateaubriand to be detected in today's writers, and more important, a deep-felt appreciation of his works on all levels of French literary society.

It is necessary, then, to break through the barrier of imperfect translation to attempt to assess the value of the man as a thinker and, to use a word dear to French critics of the author, as an *enchanter*. The word *enchanter* is particularly appropriate: what Chateaubriand gives us is not a faithful and subservient picture of reality but rather an enchantment of reality.

The student must therefore put behind him all contemporary ideas of reality and photographic representation. Chateaubriand is in many ways a kind of "primitive" in the artistic sense. Indeed, the twentieth-century novelist Julien Gracq characterizes Chateaubriand as being the Henri Rousseau of the novel. Just as Rousseau painted unacademic, primitive, and totally unrealistic pictures of the jungle, Chateaubriand attempted to transmit to the reader not a faithful and accurate representation, but rather an impression filtered through the many layers of his consciousness, deformed by his very particular vision, and subtilized in the brilliance of his own personal illumination.

Historically, Chateaubriand played important roles in three areas. In the political world he was an ambassador, cabinet minister, and statesman, and his many pamphlets in support of the principle of legitimate monarchy made him one of the outstanding supporters of the French legitimate monarchy. Except in America, where the different conditions allowed little comparison with France, Chateaubriand had slight experience with democracy, and he shared the ideas of the eighteenth-century theorists who found in the constitutional monarchy the ideal form of government. The greatest value of the monarch, according to Chateaubriand's ideas, was the absolute certainty of succession. There could be no confusion, no tumult, no chaos, only the orderly transfer of power upon the death of the executive. Obviously, this belief requires an absolute fidelity to the legitimate branch of the royal family, since the introduction of any question of choice among several possible branches of the royal house would create just that chaos which the monarchy is supposed to eliminate. Chateaubriand's adherence is, however, to a principle, not to a person. After the accession of Charles X, whom Chateaubriand considered an oppressive monarch, while still upholding the idea of legitimacy, Chateaubriand felt free to criticize severely the king who would attempt to restore the *ancien régime* in France.

In a more strictly literary field, Chateaubriand's two other important historical roles come to the fore. In 1791 Chateaubriand traveled to America, and although there is evidence that in many ways he was disappointed by what he saw in the New World, he became, through his many writings dealing with America, one of the foremost interpreters of America to the European public in the early nineteenth century. To a great extent it was through his eyes that the young Frenchman saw the fabled land of the "Savages." His view of America was often incorrect, based on faulty evidence, or even consciously falsified, but there is no question of the painting's being accepted as truth by the majority of Chateaubriand's readers.

The second great subject for which Chateaubriand was to be a spokesman was religion. It will be remembered that one of the targets of the French revolutionaries of 1789 as well as being the anathema of many of the eighteenth-century philosophers, was the established church. After the first successes of the revolution the churches were closed or turned into "temples of reason" or even used for granaries and storehouses; the convents and monasteries were dissolved; and the priests were persecuted. Once the first waves of anticlerical fervor had died down, however, religion once again began to exert its influence on the people. This was to culminate in the famous Concordat agreed to by Napoleon and the pope, re-establishing Catholicism as the state religion in France. Perhaps Napoleon was not acting exclusively out of religious considerations, since the bishops had exiled themselves, but kept in contact with the "underground" activities of the priests in France, thus serving as an effective royalist force. By gaining control of the church, Napoleon could eliminate this "subversive" element. But whatever the practical reasons, the re-establishment of relations with the church fulfilled a great need in the France of 1800.

In this same category of the historical as opposed to the esthetic interest of the author, must be placed the importance of Chateaubriand as one of the outstanding Romantics. In this way, he is at the same time a paramount example of the Romantic school of literature in France and a powerful force operating on the future development of that school.

As will be seen, one of the most fabulously successful literary works of all times was the tale *Atala*. Not far behind it comes *René*. Both works serve to typify the rising school of Romanticism: avoidance of the forms honored by the Classicists, rejection of the general and the universal in favor of the personal and the intimate, extreme reliance on individual passion and especially sentimentality as the fountainhead of literature.

René, Chateaubriand's "other self" and hero, with his languishing melancholy and unsatisfiable passions, was the model for all future Romantic heroes, literary and real.

Chateaubriand's talent as a descriptive writer added to his Romantic influence. The Romantics in general, as an outgrowth of the eighteenth-century belief in the pathetic fallacy, whereby nature was thought to be influenced by the passions of man, devoted much of their attention to nature. At every turn, Chateaubriand describes a beautiful sunset or sunrise, or he tarries to delight in a picturesque countryside. Such paintings, although not new, had never before reached such esthetic perfection.

Here too, then, Chateaubriand mirrored the tastes of his contemporaries as he guided the direction in which those tastes led.

In short, the study of these aspects of Chateaubriand can enlighten the reader on the whole of Romanticism.

All of these considerations are extremely important, and the close study of Chateaubriand would be warranted by any of them. However, they are all overshadowed by the purely esthetic value of Chateaubriand for the reader today, a value divorced entirely from any historical considerations. With no intent to study the political, social, or literary phenomena of the early nineteenth century, the reader is still faced with the incredible paradox of an author whose works were so much the product of his times but which, almost miraculously, still have profound meaning today.

The twentieth-century reader is obsessed with realism; the existence of fantasy is admissable only on a different plane from the real. Just as Molière's philosophy master in *The Would-Be Gentleman* differentiated between prose and verse by saying "What isn't prose is poetry, and what isn't poetry is prose," one tends to think today of fantasy and reality as two different and opposed phenomena. Chateaubriand, on the other hand, made no such sharp distinction. He saw no virtue in reality in itself, since he would have considered a slavish imitation of the world about him as devoid of art. The purpose of the artist, he would say, is the transposition of reality through artistic expression.

Thus, in *Atala*, Chateaubriand has to deal with the American scene. He had visited America and knew it firsthand. He had seen authentic Indians. Yet in his *Travels in America* and his other works based on the American theme, he chose to portray portions of the country he had not seen, and Indians which bore little relation to the authentic inhabitants of America. Both the scene and the actors are composed of elements drawn from imaginative travel books, from centuries of European tradition which had grown up almost to legendary proportions, and finally from Chateaubriand's own extremely fertile imagination.

The reader who accuses Chateaubriand of inaccuracies is misinterpreting the author's intentions. He knew that Indian squaws did not have long golden hair, as he describes his heroine Atala as having, and skin so white and transparent that the blue veins could be seen beneath the surface. He knew that the many and varied animals and plants he described do not occur together in the same place in nature, but he is *improving* on nature—this is the role of the artist as Chateaubriand sees it: an ordering and grouping, even a distortion, of the elements of nature, to create a wondrous and extraordinary object of beauty.

The same line of argument can be pursued in relation to Chateaubriand's undisputed masterpiece, his *Memoirs*. The reader looking for historical fact would do well to avoid the *Memoirs*. There is far more fantasy than fact in most parts of them. Why then are the *Memoirs* read? It is because they give a vision of the world which has been distilled out of the very particular conception perceived by that extraordinary personality which was Chateaubriand's.

It is true that much of Chateaubriand has lost its interest today. Of these works, little will be said except for their historical importance. Still high on the list of esthetic values, however, will be *Atala, René, The Last Abencerraje, The Martyrs, The Natchez,* and above all, the *Memoirs from Beyond the Grave.*

Acknowledgments

Acknowledgment is hereby made to Julien Gracq and Marcel Jouhandeau for their gracious permission to reproduce certain of their texts in the chapter on *The Life of Rancé*.

Contents

Contents

Chronology

1768   Chateaubriand born in Saint-Malo (September 4).

1777   Family moves to the castle of Combourg.

1786   Leaves for the army. Death of his father.

1787   Presented at Court.

1789   Fall of the Bastille. Made Knight of Malta.

1790   First work published (a minor poem).

1791   Trip to America.

1792   Louis XVI arrested at Varennes (June 22). Chateaubriand returns to France. Marriage to Céleste Buisson. Emigration.

1793-   In England.
1800

1794   Jean-Baptiste de Chateaubriand and Malesherbes family executed.

1797   *Essay on Revolutions* published.

1798   Death of mother.

1800   Returns to France.

1801   *Atala.*

1802   *Genius of Christianity.*

1803   Chateaubriand becomes secretary of the embassy at Rome.

1804   *Letter on the Roman Campagna.* Execution of the Duke d'Enghien (March 21). Death of Lucile de Chateaubriand (November 10).

1806   Trip through the Near East.

1807   Return to France.

1809   *The Martyrs.* Execution of cousin Armand de Chateaubriand (March 31).

1811   Elected to the French Academy. *Itinerary from Paris to Jerusalem.* Beginning of composition of *Memoirs.*

1814   *On Buonaparte and the Bourbons.*

1815   Napoleon's Hundred Days. Chateaubriand's exile in Ghent. Named Peer of France (August 17).

1816   *On Monarchy According to the Charter.*

1818   Founds the *Conservateur.*

1821   Minister to Berlin.

1822   Ambassador to England. Congress of Verona (September-December). Chateaubriand foreign minister (December 28).

1823   Spanish War.

1824   Relieved as foreign minister (June 6).

1825   Coronation of Charles X at Rheims.

1826- Beginning of publication of the *Complete Works* (first publica-
1827   tions of *The Natchez, The Last Abencerraje, Travels in America*).

1828   Ambassador to Rome.

1830   July Revolution; Louis-Philippe king of the French.

1831   *Historical Studies* (end of *Complete Works* in the Ladvocat edition).

1832   Arrested (June 16).

1833   First trip to Prague (May 14-June 6). Second trip to Prague (September 20-October 6).

1836   *Essay on English Literature* and translation of *Paradise Lost*. Contract for publication of the *Memoirs*.

1838   *The Congress of Verona.*

1844   *Life of Rancé.*

1847   Death of Madame de Chateaubriand.

1848   Death of Chateaubriand (July 4).

CHAPTER 1

The Life and Times of Chateaubriand

I *Importance of the Formative Years*

THE biography of Chateaubriand is perhaps more important than that of most other authors. At the same time, the life of the man explains the work and serves as the subject of a great part of it.

It is, of course, possible to consider the work entirely apart from its author in a kind of vacuum; indeed, if this were not possible, Chateaubriand would not be ranked as an important literary figure, but only as an individual of historical importance. But it is likewise true that the biographical approach to an author is of greater or lesser utility depending on the specific nature of the literary work. Obviously, if the biography is allowed to become an end in itself instead of being a means to an end, a means of reaching greater understanding of the literary figure, the technique can be worse than useless.

Chateaubriand, however, is an author who lends himself admirably to the biographical approach. First, a comparison of reality with the picture that Chateaubriand draws of himself in his works can be most enlightening concerning the author's creative processes. For the figure of Chateaubriand that we see in the works is frequently a fanciful one, the product of the author's dreams and imagination. At other times, what seems utterly fanciful in the works proves to be a faithful picturing of true events.

Moreover, Chateaubriand is a man intimately associated with his age. In every area of the work, we shall be called upon to cite Chateaubriand as utterly typical of his era, as representative of the great currents of thought and sentiment of his times. Likewise, Chateaubriand refers endlessly to all manner of persons and things which were immediately recognizable to his contemporary readers, but which the reader of today may find obscure; for example, he needs to know who is monsieur de

Malesherbes, who is Villèle, what was the Congress of Verona. It is to supply this essential background that a close examination of the life of François René[1] de Chateaubriand finds its utility.

Chateaubriand was born September 4, 1768, in Saint-Malo in Brittany. Endless numbers of critics have attempted to delineate the Celtic influence of this Breton background, and indeed the country cannot fail to leave its imprint on the individual whose formative years are spent there. In Chateaubriand's time, the Breton costume and language, both so distinctive, both setting the province so apart from the rest of France, were still strong in their traditions. Saint-Malo itself in its unique setting, a Medieval walled city almost completely surrounded by water, created a near-unique environment.

Chateaubriand was a younger son of an old and noble French family, but like so many such families, their wealth had been dissipated. Our author's immediate ancestors, however, had set about repairing the family's fortunes, culminating in his father's purchase of the chateau of Combourg, a few miles inland from Saint-Malo. The father was count of Chateaubriand, and with the purchase of the property acquired the additional title of count of Combourg. As a younger son, François René bore the title of chevalier de Combourg, a title later replaced by that of viscount de Chateaubriand.

Combourg still belongs to collateral descendants of the author, and the rooms he once inhabited are filled with memorabilia and open to visitors. The archives of the castle are still rich in documents and manuscripts pertaining to the author's life and times.

The chateau itself is perhaps one of the most significant influences in Chateaubriand's life. His early childhood was spent there, and those years left an indelible impression on him. From the *Memoirs,* it appears that Chateaubriand's father appeared to him as an awesome and terrifying person, and in fact he seems to have had some strange ways. The chateau is a fairly large medieval fortress capped with many towers and surrounded with high walls. Chateaubriand's father seems to have thought all the space in the castle must be utilized, so that the family was dispersed throughout the complex of buildings, thoroughly isolating each member from the others. Chateaubriand was born only a few years after Rousseau published his famous treatise on education, *Emile,* which is based on principles of "natural" education. Even without being a reader of Rousseau, the elder Chateaubriand might well have been convinced that this isolation of the children in his family would serve as a natural developer of independence and fortitude in his offspring.

The result, however, was quite the contrary. Left alone, François René indeed found it necessary to become self-sufficient but scarcely in the way his father would have approved. He turned in upon himself and created a state of mind which was much closer to fantasy than to reality. The perfect example of this tendency is found in the "sylphide" who reappears constantly in the *Memoirs*. The sylphide is simply the imaginary woman created in the young François René's mind, a woman representing all possible qualities and virtues to the highest degree. The still-famous ballet of *La Sylphide* had recently been created in France, which no doubt supplied Chateaubriand with the name for his love phantom. He then used the name as a magnet, drawing together impressions and emotions from all sides. He continues to such a point that the sylphide takes on a reality for him that no real woman could equal.

This process is typical of Chateaubriand and his works. Everywhere the world of fantasy and imagination take on greater consistency than the real world. Invariably, Chateaubriand's life of the imagination is more vivid than the reality that surrounds him. It is perhaps not too unrealistic to trace these attitudes to the youthful forced independence of the boy in the castle tower.

An incident of Chateaubriand's infancy is particularly interesting in the light it throws on one of the works, *Atala*. As an infant, Chateaubriand was seriously ill and near death. His nursemaid vowed that if he survived he would always be dressed in blue, the color of the Virgin. He did, of course, survive, and for some time afterward was invariably dressed in blue. But eventually it came time for him to be released from the vow, in a ceremony which was performed by the local priest. When, many years later, Chateaubriand was to have Atala's mother pronounce a similar vow, he was obviously thinking of his own experience. He was toying with the idea that such a vow is not meant to be kept, and in the natural course of events it will be obviated, as was commonly accepted by Chateaubriand's countrymen. The contrast with the Indian maid Atala, and her simplistic view of a vow which seems to be eternal, fires the artist's imagination.

François-René was sent to school in a succession of nearby institutions, religious in character for the most part, as was then customary. (Secular education in France was to begin really only with Napoleon.)

Tradition decreed a sad lot for noble younger sons. The family fortune was invariably kept intact, going from father to the eldest son, together with the property. Second and third sons could look forward to either a military or a church career. As it turned out, Chateaubriand dabbled in each of these. There was some question of his going into the church, but he had not yet undergone his "conversion," and although fervent Catholicism was no prerequisite to even high office in the church then, Chateaubriand was not enthusiastic about the prospect.

The next possibility was the navy. For some time, he waited for a commission which never arrived. The army was left. This time Chateaubriand was more fortunate, and he received his commission as second lieutenant. He did actually perform some service, interspersed, however, with long furloughs spent in Paris or Brittany. The elder Chateaubriand died while François René was on military service, whereupon Mme de Chateaubriand left the chateau to return to Saint-Malo. Thereafter, Chateaubriand was to divide his time between the army and living with his sisters.

Of his sisters, Lucile was certainly the favorite. She was somewhat of a literary turn of mind, and a few of her poems have been preserved. She was her brother's confidante and adviser. She is clearly discernable under the portrait of Amélie in *René*, and many of the sentiments and scenes depicted in the novel resemble the actual circumstances. The idea of incestuous love, however, seems much more likely to be the result of a literary influence than based on fact. Even a rapid glance at the novels being written at the time of *René* will show that incest was one of the populalr literary subjects of the day.

Lucile was to become a canoness in a holy order but hardly under the circumstances of Amélie in the novel. Lucile's convent was anything but cloistered; it admitted only those young ladies of ancient and very noble lineage, and acceptance in the order conferred the title of countess.

Chateaubriand, at least to judge by the sentiments painted in the *Memoirs*, was still shy and reticent at this time. It was through the insistence of his brother, therefore, and for reasons of family advancement, that he agreed to allow himself to be presented at court. The scene is described in detail in the *Memoirs*, although some of the detail is questionable. After his levee, the king entered the oeil-de-beouf room in the Palace of Versailles, where he was presented to Chateaubriand. Chateaubriand then rushed into the Hall of Mirrors to pay his respects to Marie-Antoinette as she passed, returning from the chapel to her apartments. The next ceremony was attending the king's hunt. Apparently, Chateaubriand committed the unforgivable sin of reaching the prey before the king. According to which of two existing versions of the scene one chooses to believe, either the king was furious or he magnanimously pardoned the young offender.

The ceremonies finished, Chateaubriand immediately left Versailles, never again to see Louis XVI and Marie-Antoinette, until many years later when he was made a member of a commission attempting to identify the bodies of the royal family, exhumed from the common grave into which they had been cast after their execution.

In this society moving so rapidly toward revolution, Chateaubriand continued to play the traditional role of the young nobleman. Just as his father had continued to receive feudal tribute at Combourg, Chateaubriand was prevailed upon to become a Knight of Malta. The same proof of ancient nobility that had made Lucile eligible to be canoness sufficed for Chateaubriand as a Knight of Malta. The title was not only honorific but brought with it a sizable income, which was of course a prime concern for the young soldier.

II *The Revolution*

Chateaubriand was in Paris at the time of the events leading up to the taking of the Bastille in 1789. One scene he describes in particular portrayed the procession of a group of revolutionaries up the street in which he lived: two severed heads impaled on spikes were being carried at the head of the triumphal parade. Chateaubriand was to witness many such events, and through his friends and family he was to know of many more.

From this brutal confrontation was to come the basic paradox of Chateaubriand's political attitude. His attitudes were basically liberal, in spite of his aristocratic background (as was the case with many others, such as Lafayette). He was certainly no friend of absolutism, but there soon was to be no middle ground between the extremist revolutionaries and the monarchists. Later, the constitutional monarchy of Louis XVIII was to be, in theory at least, Chateaubriand's ideal, but the practicalities of the situation soon disenchanted him.

At the moment, however, Chateaubriand could not find it possible to support either cause wholeheartedly. It was at this point that he seems to have started dreaming of "far-away places" with the idea of combining his desire to travel with the most judicious course of action for a young nobleman at such a point in French history.

In 1790 there took place in Paris a great celebration, the Feast of the Federation, a kind of apotheosis of the new order. It was the first anniversary of the taking of the Bastille, and it seemed to be the moment of conciliation between the revolutionary leaders and those of the church together with the king. One of the high points of the celebration was a mass said by that extraordinary man, Talleyrand, who managed to serve all regimes from the monarchy through the republic to the empire, in all capacities from bishop to cabinet minister.

Obviously such an event must be carefully described in the *Memoirs* unless there is a reason to the contrary. However, Chateaubriand passes rapidly over the feast saying he was ill and could not attend. Actually, patient scholars have discovered that, in fact, Chateaubriand was not in Paris at the time. But for him to reveal the reason for his absence would have been humiliating to his vanity and out of tone with the *Memoirs*.

The fact is that somehow Chateaubriand had contracted a large debt, which he was liquidating by selling stockings to members of his regiment: it was this business that kept him away from Paris at the time of the feast—a minor incident, to be sure, and its suppression is almost childish. However, it deserves attention as an example of the author's habitual method of speaking of himself, a method which was again intended to maintain a lofty tone, especially in the area of appearances, so important for Chateaubriand for whom realities take second place to appearances and fantasy.

Chateaubriand's regiment was now stationed at Rouen. The various regiments around France were going through crises of disaffection. So far, Chateaubriand's Navarre Regiment had held firm, but now the cracks began to show there too. Incidents which provoked a confrontation between the military and the Rouen populace caused insurrection in the ranks, as it had caused elsewhere. No longer sure of the troops, the commander, Mortemart (a nobleman of one of the oldest families of France), and his senior officers, decided to emigrate. A decision was forced on Chateaubriand. He reached a decision which was no decision by simply resigning from the regiment: "I had neither adopted nor rejected the new opinions; equally indisposed to attack them or to serve them, I wished neither to emigrate nor to continue my military career: I withdrew" (*Memoirs,* V. 15).[2]

Chateaubriand was thus left without a profession and without income, and, more important, without interests and goals. His brother had married the granddaughter of monsieur de Malesherbes, and it was he, apparently with the encouragement of the Chateaubriand family, who inspired the young man with the idea of going to America.

III *Trip to America*

There has been much discussion among the critics concerning the purpose of the trip. The idea Chateaubriand himself indicates is an attempt to discover the Northwest Passage. Many have thought this was a pretext and an afterthought, but there is evidence to show that he had discussed this purpose with different persons before he made the voyage. It is quite obvious from his writings that even after making the trip he had no real idea of the vast distances to be covered in America, so the idea of a trip of discovery might have seemed entirely logical to him at the time.

In fact, however, he found himself with nothing to do, and France was not a good place for a young nobleman to be in 1790. He had already been interested in travel. What more logical than an extended journey? Chance seems to have dictated America. Again we find one of the great influences on the life and works of Chateaubriand. The details of the trip and the controversy surrounding it will be examined in the chapter on Chateaubriand's America (Chapter 5). We shall give only an outline of the trip here.

Early in 1791 he went to Saint-Malo, perhaps not the most likely port for finding a ship to take him to America; the choice was no doubt dictated by the fact that his mother was still living there. After some time, arrangements were made for Chateaubriand to make this crossing on a tiny cod-fishing brigantine which had been chartered to take a few clerics to Baltimore where a new seminary was to be founded. The ship left Saint-Malo June 8, 1791. After stops in the Azores, at the French island of Saint-Pierre off the Newfoundland coast, and on the Virginia coast, the travelers arrived in Baltimore July 10. Chateaubriand disembarked, stayed overnight, and left by stagecoach the next morning for Philadelphia.

Philadelphia was the national capital in 1791, and it was there that Chateaubriand attempted to see George Washington. He had a letter of introduction from Colonel Armand, a French comrade in arms of Washington from the revolutionary days, but Washington was ill and could not receive him; this was, of course, a situation impossible to describe and still preserve Chateaubriand's ego, and the *Travels in America* and the *Memoirs* describe an imaginary interview with the president and later an imaginary dinner at the presidential mansion.

Chateaubriand, again traveling by stagecoach, headed for New York City. From there he says he went to Boston and visited the battlefield of Lexington, then returned to New York, but there is little to substantiate this "side-trip." He sailed up the Hudson to Albany, where he engaged a Dutch guide to lead him to Niagara. As he followed the Mohawk trail, he no doubt came into contact with many Indians; the European settlements were still very scattered, and much of the region was wilderness. However, the scenes of meetings with Indians and Europeans that he describes in his works are probably only partly true if they are not completely imaginary.

He arrived at Niagara and presumably spent some time there, especially if, as he repeatedly says, he broke his arm and had to wait for it to heal. From this point, it is impossible to establish a solid itinerary for the traveler. He says, or at times implies, in his works, that he had visited virtually all of America east of the Mississippi, from north to south. Obviously he did not, since there was not enough time at his disposal.

In all probability he traveled in a leisurely fashion back toward the east coast, by canoe, horseback, or a combination of both. According to his own description, as he neared the east coast he picked up an old newspaper and learned the news of the French king's flight to Varennes.[3] This is probably factual, as the newspaper headline he quotes is authentic.

His honor was calling him back to France, so he took the first available ship from Philadelphia for Le Havre, arriving there in early January after a great storm at sea. One might be tempted to speculate that this call of honor was merely a pretext, since Chateaubriand had not previously shown any overwhelming sense of duty to the crown. However, a look at the circumstances does indeed make this seem logical.

The Feast of the Federation has been mentioned. At that time in 1790, there seemed to be an appearance of movement toward restored order. The king played an important part in the feast, and, disagreeable as he and the aristocrats might have found the situation forced upon them, there did indeed seem to be a possibility of reconciliation. The king went so far as to wear a giant tricolor cockade in his hat to show his sympathy (willing or unwilling) with the revolutionary cause.

However, the last news Chateaubriand had had before his departure from France had been a letter from Paris announcing the death of the moderate Mirabeau, an ominous event for those who sought an end to the violence.

But when the king decided, together with his immediate family, to flee from Paris in an attempt to reach Belgium and safety, he sounded the death knell for his whole family. They were recognized and arrested before they could reach safety and were brought back to Paris as prisoners. All the sympathy they may have had and all of the tolerance their enemies had shown was gone. Chateaubriand could thus realize that the situation had changed drastically. It is easy to understand how a young man, until then uncommitted, could suddenly reach a crucial decision.

IV *Emigration and Exile*

Back in France, personal problems arose for Chateaubriand. He had no money. His transatlantic passage had still not been paid for, and he had to borrow the money to pay the captain. The financial advantages of his role as Knight of Malta had disappeared, the ecclesiastical benefices reverting to the revolutionary government, and of course the feudal income from Combray had likewise disappeared. He could not even emigrate to join the royalist army in Germany without money to pay his way. The answer was marriage. The families arranged a marriage with the seventeen-year-old Celeste Buisson. Chateaubriand was twenty-four.

The marriage ceremony was as romanesque as any Romantic could hope. The elder Mme de Chateaubriand insisted that the marriage be performed by a "refractory" priest. Part of the arrangement forced upon the church by the revolutionary government had been a requirement that all the priests sign a loyalty oath to the new regime. Those who refused were counted outlaws and deprived of the civil right to perform any ceremonies. The young couple was therefore forced to be married in secret by a priest who had refused the oath. But since such a marriage could not be recognized in civil law, a second ceremony was required by a "sworn priest."

The new Mme de Chateaubriand turned out to have less of a fortune than had been thought, so that the myriad financial troubles were magnified rather than solved. Some bitter reflections on married life can be seen in the *Memoirs,* and these seem certainly the result of the pecuniary difficulties. On the whole, however, there appeared to be mutual regard and respect. There were to be no children of the marriage. Chateaubriand in the *Memoirs* seems to hint that the fault was his. At any rate, Mme de Chateaubriand was to spend many lonely hours, with no children to occupy her and with her husband away visiting one of his many lady friends, not unknown to her. The result was that she involved herself passionately in charitable works.

She had a role to play in Chateaubriand's work, however. She occasionally acted as his secretary, taking down portions of the *Memoirs* as Chateaubriand dictated them. She read portions of the *Memoirs* and made suggestions. Above all, she composed a series of remembrances, at the request of her husband, which he used to refresh his memory in composing the *Memoirs.*

The political situation was becoming more dangerous by the day, and finally on July 15, 1792, Chateaubriand made the break and emigrated. His plan was to join the "Army of the Princes" at Coblenz. The émigré nobles had gathered there to launch a counterrevolution, an enterprise which Chateaubriand later joined in characterizing as the "folly of Coblenz." He made his way through Lille, Brussels, Coblenz, and finally Trier. His cousin Armand found it necessary to use all his influence to make it possible for Chateaubriand to join the army. Perhaps his late arrival cast suspicion on him; perhaps his tardiness merely struck the earlier arrivals as an eleventh-hour commitment.

At any rate, he was eventually admitted to the Breton Regiment. His original army service had been in the Navarre Regiment, but in this moment of tested loyalties, the soldiers were grouped in general according to their native provinces.

This Army of the Princes was a curious army. It consisted entirely of officers, but since there were no longer any enlisted men in the ranks, the officers filled the role of privates. They lived in tents and took turns doing the menial duties. Chateaubriand boasted of his ability as a cook when his turn would come around: "I was marvelous at preparing the mess."

Chateaubriand did enjoy some leisure, however, and much of this he employed in writing. If we are to believe what he tells us, everywhere he went he carried with him an enormous pack filled with manuscript. He had plenty of room, as most of his clothing and belongings had been stolen. In looking back on those days, Chateaubriand frequently spoke of this manuscript and its various parts, referring in particular to *Atala*. The exact state of the manuscript seems to be difficult to determine, however. As far as we can tell, Chateaubriand wrote constantly, editing and rewriting, adding new material and developments to a huge manuscript which was to be a kind of reservoir from which he was to draw much of his later material. Therefore, although the celebrated work to be published under the title of *Atala* certainly existed in some form long before its publication in 1801, it is difficult to say whether it existed in 1792 as a relatively coherent story or whether it was merely a series of sketches.

Finally military duties called, and the Army of the Princes marched on the city of Thionville to lay siege to it. In the course of the battle, Chateaubriand was wounded in the leg by shrapnel, and he discovered later that his pack had received a bullet, but the mass of manuscript had protected its author. "Atala, as a dutiful daughter, put herself between her father and the enemy lead" (*Memoirs*, 15).

On top of the aftereffects of the leg wound, Chateaubriand fell ill with dysentery, referred to as "the Prussian disease." The army as a whole had come on hard times, and there was a general releasing of men, supposedly temporary, but which eventually became permanent. Therefore, the invalid was free to make his way back. In addition to other ills, he then came down with what is described as smallpox, but which may have been a serious case of chicken pox. Whatever the disease, it was to leave his face pockmarked, as can be seen by the description on the passport which was later issued to him. A touch of vanity can be seen in the *Memoirs,* where Chateaubriand quotes the passport description in the text, but eliminates the reference to the pockmarks.

Hobbling with a crutch, he made his way painfully through the Ardennes forest until he reached Brussels, where he found his brother who took him in charge and loaned him enough money to see him through. The brother then returned to France. Chateaubriand first planned to return to Brittany; Brittany and Vendée were the two areas most hostile to the revolutionaries, and the leaders of the new regime did not yet have the overwhelming strength that they possessed in Paris and the rest of France. Still, there was considerable danger involved, and Chateaubriand, strongly advised to change his plans, decided instead on exile in England.

So he made his way to Ostend where he found a boat for the Channel Islands. His health was so bad, however, that the captain of the boat was unwilling to take him all the way to his destination in Jersey and put him ashore to die in Guernsey. The locals found him and cared for him, however, and he was able to reach Jersey, where the Bedée family, relations of his mother, were in exile.

He needed four months for an even partial recovery. His thoughts again turned to Brittany, but once more he was advised to continue to England. The French atmosphere of Jersey might have been more agreeable, but money was a problem. The Bedée family had enough to do to support themselves without an additional mouth to feed. England seemed to offer more opportunities.

Thus, he continued his journey, landing at Southampton and then heading for London. Here his precarious health deteriorated even more, and the doctors pronounced his illness fatal. Feeling as if he were racing with time, he began the writing of his *Essay on Revolutions,* making use of the research facilities of the British Museum and of several private libraries. To support himself, he worked as a literary translator during the days, devoting his evenings to the writing of the *Essay.*

In 1794 he moved to the small town of Beccles, near Norwich, northeast of London, to teach French in schools and in private lessons. He may also have gone there to work on some Old French manuscripts for a collector. This last reason is the only one given by Chateaubriand himself—he obviously wanted to hide what he considered the humiliation of having to give lessons. It is not clear whether the manuscript work was a fabrication or not.

This was a particularly difficult time for the author. Although he had confounded the doctors by recovering his health, the family was in tragic circumstances. Chateaubriand's brother had been adjudged a traitor for having emigrated, and he and his wife, Chateaubriand's sister-in-law and granddaughter of the old friend Malesherbes, as well as Malesherbes himself, had been executed. Chateaubriand's mother had been taken to prison in Paris, and his wife and sister Lucile had been imprisoned in Rennes. They were saved from execution only by the amnesty of the 9 Thermidor (July 27, 1794) date of the overthrow of Robespierre and the end of the Reign of Terror.

Nearby the town of Beccles is Bungay, destined to rival Combourg as the scene of important events in the author's life. There he made the acquaintance of a local churchman with a young daughter: Charlotte Ives. The two young people were immediately drawn to one another. They spent endless hours together talking and studying. Although he was long past the age, Chateaubriand was much in the situation he describes for his character René. (See the chapter on *The Genius of Christianity* where the passage on "The Vagueness of passions" is given.) He was full of desire but had not yet met the individual who could respond to those desires. The woman of his dreams remained in his dreams, the Sylphide of his youth. Suddenly he found the person who matched the dreams—Charlotte. Chateaubriand said of her: "Since that time, I have met with only one attachment exalted enough to inspire me with the same confidence" (*Memoirs,* X, 9). The second attachment was to be, of course, the long and enduring friendship with Madame Récamier.

The family of Charlotte Ives was not blind to what was happening. Persuaded that their daughter would be happy with Chateaubriand, they proposed a marriage. Suddenly Chateaubriand's dream world vanished. He had to admit that he was already married, and, feeling he had betrayed the hospitality if not the honor of the Ives family, he rushed back to London.

V *First Writings*

All this time he had been working steadily on his *Essay*, and it was finally ready for publication in 1797. The full title is: *Historical, Political and Ethical Essay on Ancient and Modern Revolutions, Considered in Their Relation to the French Revolution*. The title seems vast enough, but the subject matter is even more all-embracing: "The Essay offers the compendium of my existence as poet, moralist, publicist and politician" (*Memoirs* XI, 2). Side by side with the historical portions are materials of the most disparate nature, including descriptions of his trip to America, which indeed have little to do with the subject. The author was still under the Rousseauistic philosophical influence, and he had not yet fully embraced the principle of constitutional monarchy that was to guide his later years.

Today, the interest of the *Essay* is mainly historical, although as with so many of Chateaubriand's works, a few "anthology pages" count among his masterpieces of description.

The work had little success, although it did serve to enhance his reputation to a degree, since he was now a bona fide published author. From a financial point of view, however, it was not a profitable venture, and the penury of Chateaubriand's life in England continued, hardly abated by the one-shilling-per-day dole given to the French émigrés.

At the end of May, Chateaubriand's mother died. This seems to have provoked some kind of moral crisis in Chateaubriand resulting in his "conversion" or rather his return to the Catholic Church. But this was to be far more than a personal concern, because the conversion was to be the inspiration for one of the most influential works ever published: *The Genius of Christianity*. As with the *Essay*, there was an all-embracing subject, partly historical, partly literary, partly descriptive, which was to be a great apology for the Christian religion; this was to be developed by an examination not only of its values but also its unrealized potentialities. The work in its definitive form was not to be published, however, until 1802.

Meanwhile, the succession of revolutionary governments in France had ended in the Consulat, with Napoleon Bonaparte as first consul. The Reign of Terror had been over for many years, and France was returning to some kind of normalcy. The result was a mass return of the émigrés. Chateaubriand was among those who chose now to return, and in 1800 he once more set foot on French soil.

However, this return was far from normal for Chateaubriand himself. He was still an émigré noble, an enemy of the state, a conspirator. Therefore, he found it necessary to return under an assumed name. Of course, a concerted police effort could certainly have unmasked Chateaubriand, but there was a kind of relaxation of the tensions at this time, and the young author, while still having to maintain an official fiction of being someone else, was in no real danger.

From England he brought with him many of the manuscripts on which he had been working, although he had to leave some behind, in a trunk in his former lodgings. Among those he brought was the beginning of *The Genius of Christianity* which the author hoped to be able to publish in the near future. But day-to-day needs required some support, and Chateaubriand's old friend Fontanes arranged for a position as writer on the well-known journal, the *Mercure,* which had a reputation for controversy. Chateaubriand was to have a close association with this journal until it was banned by Napoleon a few years later.

It soon appeared that the *Genius* would not soon be ready for publication. In trying to determine his best course of action, Chateaubriand had a brilliant idea, one that was to affect his career to an enormous extent: he would publish one of the episodes of the *Genius* by itself. Thus it was that in 1801 appeared *Atala,* an "Indian" tale vaguely inspired by his travels in America and by his readings. The story was to serve as the illustration of one of Chateaubriand's principles stated in the parent work: the classical subjects of the ancients should be abandoned and be replaced by stories growing out of Christianity.

There are not many examples of such immediate and total success of a work of literature as in the case of *Atala.* From a penniless émigré hiding behind an assumed name, Chateaubriand suddenly became the proverbial toast of Paris literary society. He now had influential friends not only on the literary scene but in Napoleon's own family. Together, Mme de Staël and Elise Bonaparte arranged to have the name of Chateaubriand removed from the official list of émigrés.

Riding on the wave of intense popularity created by *Atala,* Chateaubriand finished the work on the *Genius,* publishing it the following year, 1802. Again the effect was enormous. The religious subject was extremely appropriate to the times: during the revolutionary years, religion was outlawed, convents and monasteries were dissolved, churches were abandoned. It was soon clear to Bonaparte, however, that religion could not be stamped out among the French populace. The result was an "underground" religious movement, closely allied with the émigré bishops of the *ancien régime.* Largely as a practical measure, then, Bonaparte found it necessary to re-establish official Catholicism with a hierarchy loyal to him. This was the background of Napoleon's Concordat with the pope. The Concordat was signed on April 8, 1801. Chateaubriand's *Genius* appeared on April 14. As with so many of his works, it was completely in tune with the times. Although it was greatly influenced by current ideas, the work also had enormous influence on the further development of those ideas.

Certainly one of the most important and influential books in the whole history of ideas in France, the work was designed to paint the moral and esthetic beauties of Christianity, extolling the pictorial fascination of the liturgy itself and at the same time illustrating the resources Christianity offers in the way of literary inspiration. The *Genius* is examined more closely in Chapter 3.

From this time onward, Chateaubriand enjoyed the reputation of being the defender of Christianity. In the *Memoirs* we frequently see the scene in which Chateaubriand, traveling in a foreign country, is received with enthusiasm by the locals who invariably rush up to meet this defender of religion. Such a reputation has naturally given rise to an extended controversy as to Chateaubriand's own religious convictions. Was he acting in good faith, or was he merely being the opportunist seizing upon the popular subject of the day? The answer to the controversy is made more difficult by the very particular conception of religion on the author's part, and by the early *philosophe-*oriented writings. A balanced appraisal would seem to show that after a traditional Catholic upbringing the young René was rather casual in his attitude toward religion. However, the many tragedies of the revolutionary period seem indeed to have returned him to a fervent faith. But this religion of his is not a cerebral religion dealing with abstractions. Religion for Chateaubriand has basically an appeal to the emotions, complete with visual beauty, sentimentality, and above all, the overwhelming power of associations. To him, the paramount value of religion seems to be its power to inspire reverie, to cause reflection, to create a kind of immortality in its capacity to weld together emotions that span the centuries.

Once again, the increased literary reputation had its social consequences. The old chateaux of the nobility were being reopened and a new salon life instituted. Chauteaubriand was welcomed into these milieux, where he was to make influential friends, but where, more importantly, he was to find an everincreasing literary forum which would be most useful in the development of his literary and philosophical views.

VI *Embassy Post in Rome and the Break with Napoleon*

More important, his celebrity now brought him to the attention of Napoleon. The future emperor decided to make use of the young author's talents by naming him secretary of the embassy in Rome. The trip there and his stay were to form the basis of some of Chateaubriand's minor works, *Travels in Italy*, one portion of which remains one of the greatest stylistic achievements of the author, the *Letter to Fontanes on the Roman Countryside*.

In Rome, Chateaubriand was visited by one of his friends, another of the several very influential women in his life, Pauline de Beaumont. She was dying of one of those poetic diseases of the nineteenth century, which caused her gradually to waste away. Modern readers are sometimes annoyed by the frequency of such deaths in the literature of the period. The literature, however, does nothing but mirror the actual state of affairs. As each age overcomes a major cause of death, a new disease comes to replace it. Both in literature and actuality, however, the nineteenth-century wasting away had undeniable poetic value, especially in the age when esthetics still decreed that a beautiful literary portrait must begin with a beautiful subject.

At any rate, Pauline de Beaumont's visit was a farewell one. The depth of Chateaubriand's feelings can be judged from the description he gives in the *Memoirs*:

The good that the air of Rome had done Madame de Beaumont was not lasting: the signs of immediate deterioration disappeared, it is true, but it always seems as if this last moment is prolonged only to deceive us. Two or three times I had tried a carriage outing with the invalid; I sought to interest her by drawing her attention to the sky or the landscape; she no longer took pleasure in anything. One day, I took her to the Coliseum; it was one of those October days you find only in Rome. She managed to get out of the carriage, and went to sit on a stone, facing one of the altars placed around the edge of the building. She lifted her eyes; she slowly looked over the porticos, themselves dead for so many years, and which had seen so much death; the ruins were decorated with briars and ranunculus which autumn had sprinkled with saffron, and which were bathed in light. The dying woman lowered her gaze, following the descending levels down to the arena, her eyes avoiding the sun; she fixed her gaze on the cross of the altar, and said to me: "Let us go; I am cold." I took her back home; she went to bed, never to get up again. (XV, 4)

In 1804 Chateaubriand was due for a promotion. Napoleon named him ambassador to the Valais, now one of the federated cantons of Switzerland. Chateaubriand's satisfaction was short-lived, however. Early that year the duke d'Enghien[4] had been captured by Napoleon's police (who for that purpose had violated German territory). He was now tried, and found guilty, and executed.

The killing had symbolic importance. Closely identified with the *ancien régime,* the duke was a member of a collateral line of the Bourbons. His family had served France as military leaders for centuries. The execution was meant as an object lesson. To one of Chateaubriand's background, it could be only the most insolent of crimes, and he immediately resigned his diplomatic post, leaving no doubt as to the reason.

Those who would detract from Chateaubriand's character often try to paint his as a vainglorious little man, given to absurd gestures. However given to gestures Chateaubriand might be, they were always made in support of a principle, and often, as in this case, involved certain very definite personal risks. Many would have grumbled in silence or would have imitated Talleyrand in eschewing all principles in order to serve every changing regime.

Chateaubriand was left with time on his hands. This inactivity was charged with sadness when his sister Lucile died. On the other hand, Mme de Chateaubriand could ill-conceal her relief at her sister-in-law's death. Apparently Lucile had enormously complicated life for Mme de Chateaubriand (and indeed, modern critics see in Lucile a definite neurotic, even from the early days at Combourg). For Chateaubriand, however, this was another cruel personal blow.

VII *Trip to the Orient*

To fill the void, he determined on a trip to the Middle East. He had for some time wished to build upon his theory of the value of Christian inspiration in literature, and he intended to write an epic centered around the Christians martyred at the hands of the Roman emperor Diocletian. For this he felt a visit to the scenes of his story was of prime necessity.

He set out in July, 1806, leaving Mme de Chateaubriand behind in Europe. Perhaps he did not feel that Céleste was the best of traveling companions, but she may very well have been left behind for purely practical reasons. After all, Mr. Cook had not yet appeared on the scene to organize his tours, and the dangers of Middle East travel afforded then by robbers, disease, war, and religious fanaticism should not be underestimated.

Chateaubriand visited Egypt and the Holy Land and then returned to France through Spain, not arriving home until 1807. Through a series of circumstances, he then found himself sole proprietor of the *Mercure* with which he had been associated since his return from exile. He made use of his journal to protest again the execution of the duke d'Enghien, an event which was still far from forgotten. Napoleon was furious at Chateaubriand's article and immediately closed down the paper.

The trip to Jerusalem had cost a fortune. The closing of the *Mercure* created more financial difficulties. A final blow to Chateaubriand's precarious financial position was the purchase of a house, La Vallée-aux-Loups, a short distance outside Paris. This was one of Chateaubriand's most precious possessions. He loved the location and there indulged himself in all sorts of poetic fancies (such as planting an American magnolia tree). He was destined to lose the house, however: "of all things I have lost, the only one I miss" (*Memoirs*, XVIII, 5).

The idea of writing his memoirs had occurred to him earlier, but here at La Vallée-aux-Loups he began work in earnest, a work that was to occupy him until shortly before his death— and a work that was to become one of the world's undoubted literary masterpieces. At this time, too, was completed the famous Girodet painting of Chateaubriand which is such a magnificent representation of the Romantic attitude and temperament.

The Middle East epic, *The Martyrs,* was finally ready and was published in 1809. The criticism was harsh from many of the critics. However, the work was gradually to attain a most respectable position having been reprinted almost continuously to the present.

The year 1809 brought another personal tragedy. Chateaubriand's cousin Armand had been arrested in January. Armand had taken a politically active part in the opposition to the Republic; he was convicted as an enemy of the state and executed by firing squad in front of the Paris city walls. In his *Memoirs,* Chateaubriand adds the gruesome detail that after the execution a butcher's dog came to lap up the blood and eat the brains of the victim (*Memoirs,* XVIII, 7).

VIII *Literary Successes and Political Activities*

Chateaubriand returned to his writing, this time preparing a travel book based on his trip to the Near East. This was published in 1811. By this time his literary reputation was so firmly established that he was encouraged to present himself for election as a member of the Institute. He was indeed elected, but his chair was that vacated by the death of the critic and dramatist Marie-Joseph Chénier, who as a member of the Convention had voted in favor of death for Louis XVI. For his acceptance speech, Chateaubriand wrote a resounding condemnation of the regicide. However, he was not allowed to present it: it was censored by Napoleon.

While Napoleon was occupied with his Russian adventure, Chateaubriand was busy writing an anti-Bonapartist pamphlet, *On Buonaparte and the Bourbons,* using the Italianate spelling of Bonaparte as a calculated insult. Poor Mme de Chateaubriand was positively terrified at the possible consequences if the authorities discovered what Chateaubriand was doing. She was sure he would be hanged for treason. In 1814, with the anti-Napoleonic forces at the very gates of Paris, Chateaubriand decided to have the pamphlet secretly printed. When Napoleon had been defeated and forced to abdicate, Chateaubriand might have well expected great honors from the restored King Louis XVIII. The honors were not forthcoming.

From this point, Chateaubriand seems to have developed a feeling of persecution or at least ingratitude on the part of the Bourbons. They did not seem to be ready to reward the staunch supporter of royalty with the respect he felt was due him.

At any rate, Chateaubriand continued to associate with the people of the court, outstanding among these being the duchess of Duras. She was an extremely intelligent woman of society and a penetrating writer who did a great deal to influence Chateaubriand personally and literarily in the following years.

Finally, a suitable "reward" for Chateaubriand's support was found: he was named ambassador to Sweden. Unfortunately, he was destined never to have the chance to assume the post. The king of Sweden was Napoleon's former lieutenant Bernadotte, who had been invited to come to Sweden as king. The reputation of Chateaubriand as a politician was based on the Bonaparte pamphlet, the thrust of which was to demonstrate that only the "legitimate," hereditary, undoubted king could rule effectively. He was arguing against Napoleon, but the arguments were equally applicable to Bernadotte. Apparently, the Swedish king wanted no defender of royal legitimacy as ambassador, when he himself was not a legitimate king.

Before the matter could be settled, Napoleon was back from Elba. Louis XVIII immediately fled in terror, followed by most of the court, including M. and Mme de Chateaubriand. The dismay of Paris at seeing the emperor return is described with a certain wry humor by Chateaubriand in the *Memoirs*.[5]

Chateaubriand's great political activity dates from this period. First he was named a minister in the government in exile. Later, after Napoleon's defeat in 1815, he served as an election commissioner; finally, he was named Peer of France, which gave him the right to sit in the Chamber of Peers. There he was to play a leading role, at times speaking in favor of the government, at times in the opposition, but never hesitating to declare his frank sentiments in often inflammatory speeches.

In his rather quixotic way, Chateaubriand seemed more at home as a member of the opposition than as a supporter. This has fascinated the critics who have attempted to prove either that Chateaubriand had no political convictions or that he was a simple opportunist. The truth seems to be that his nature required him to attack what he thought needed attacking, regardless of the government. Thus, he could uphold the principle of monarchy and attack certain of its foundations at the same time, without contradiction. This is what he did in his 1816 pamphlet, *On Monarchy According to the Charter,* in which he gave his ideas on the exact nature that he felt a constitutional monarchy should assume. But his ideas did not coincide with those of the government, and the book was seized, although later returned. As a result of the pamphlet, Chateaubriand was soon after removed from his post as one of the ministers of state (minister without portfolio). The loss of the minister's stipend made it necessary for him to sell not only his library but the beloved house at La Vallée-aux-Loups.

Officially out of the government, Chateaubriand assumed the position of one of the leaders of the opposition, both in the legislature and in the journalistic world. He founded a journal called *The Conservative* which for two years served as a voice for the opposition until it was closed by the censors.

One of the most notorious events of the period involved the duke de Berry. He was in line for the throne as son of the future King Charles X. In 1820 the duke was assassinated on the steps of the Opera House. His wife was awaiting the birth of a child. The son, the duke of Bordeaux, "the miracle child" as the posthumous son was called, would be the legitimate heir to the throne, and Chateaubriand was to consider him as "Henry V" after the abdication of Charles X, in spite of the fact that Louis-Philippe actually became king.

It is difficult to say just how much these romantic circumstances attached Chateaubriand even more firmly to the "legitimate" elder branch of the reigning family, but certainly they played their role. Despite rebuffs, Chateaubriand would continue to serve Louis XVIII, then later Charles X and his family, including the duchess of Berry, even in their later exile.

Chateaubriand was named ambassador to Berlin in 1821, and his stipend as minister of state was restored to him. Although very successful as ambassador, he felt it necessary to resign during a political shakeup; however, he was soon named ambassador to England, where he took up his duties in 1822, without Mme de Chateaubriand, however, since she feared the perils of crossing the channel.

In England the diplomatic success continued. Chateaubriand moved easily with royalty and political figures. His receptions at the embassy became famous, owing in no small part to the skill of his cook. His steaks became so well known that the name of Chateaubriand was given to that particular cut most favored.

Important political events overshadowed the social events, however. Spain was troubled with revolution at home and in the colonies. The main concern to France was the danger of having a Bourbon monarch (King Ferdinand was related to Louis XVIII) deposed by the revolutionaries: the French might copy the move in France. Other nations, particularly England, were unwilling however to risk a war on this account. The result was the Congress of Verona, called to make plans and decide on a course of action. Chateaubriand was one of the members of the French delegation and played an important role in it. Some of the details of this situation will be examined in Chapter 6. Suffice it to say here that Chateaubriand and his party won out, and France decided on armed intervention to restore Ferdinand to his throne.

Instead of being returned to London, Chateaubriand was made foreign minister, prime director of the Spanish adventure. The result, rapidly achieved, was victory and restoration of Ferdinand. But the original dissensions still persisted, and, the war faction losing influence, Chateaubriand was rather unceremoniously removed as foreign minister in June, 1824.

Money problems arose again, and Chateaubriand had the idea of solving them with an edition of his complete works, which would contain a great deal of unpublished material (*The Natchez, Travels in America,* among others). The publication venture was begun in 1826, but it did not prove to be the profit-making affair the author had hoped. Nevertheless, the edition was to require an enormous amount of the author's time. Mme de Chateaubriand, meanwhile, was becoming more and more invovled in her charitable works that were to occupy her for the rest of her life.

On the death of Louis XVIII, his brother, Charles X, had replaced him. At one time, during a ministerial crisis, Chateaubriand had been approached with the possibility of rejoining the cabinet, but his feelings were still bruised. After the "insult" of his removal, he would return only if reinstated as foreign minister, which was not the post being offered him.

The post which did tempt him, however, was the ambassadorship to Rome. The nostalgia of his early days there as secretary to the Embassy, together with Rome's overpowering historical and literary associations, were too strong to be denied. He accepted the post as France's representative at the court of Pope Leo XII. It was a difficult post because there were controversies in France over the recent government actions which had given greater secular controls over church schools. However, Chateaubriand found a friend in the pope, and the round of high-level entertaining continued. Mme de Chateaubriand was particularly happy to be able to have "all the cardinals of Christendom" at her house for dinner.

All this was cut short by the death of the pope in early 1829. Immediately there began the machinations of the powerful to influence the choice of the new pope. Chateaubriand was to be intimately involved in these activities. He perhaps did not hesitate, in his writings, to magnify his own role in the election, to the point of speaking of "my pope," but he was certainly a powerful force felt in the conclave. Chateaubriand was particularly anxious to promote the election of a pope favorable to France's interests. The result of the conclave, the election of Pius VIII, was indeed favorable to France, although the Austrian interests were soothed by the choice of papal secretary of state.

In spite of the exalted position of ambassador, Chateaubriand continued to have money troubles. According to the practice of the day, the ambassador was expected to set up his own establishment, going into debt if necessary, so that the first year of an ambassadorship had to be counted as a pure loss. Only after three years, according to Chateaubriand, could an ambassador expect to make ends meet. Once again he seems to have been destined to experience one of those serious disappointments that kept coming on the heels of his success. After his advantageous maneuvering in Rome, he was expecting to be brought back into the cabinet; but when he returned to Paris on leave in mid-1829, he was surprised to be given a rather cool reception. Events were fast moving toward the July revolution, and in a vain attempt to stem the tide, the cabinet had been overturned and replaced by a new one headed by Polignac. This was the same man whom Chateaubriand as foreign minister had strongly supported as ambassador to England. But as prime minister, he was unacceptable to Chateaubriand, representing as he did an antiliberal viewpoint. Chateaubriand immediately resigned his ambassadorship in protest, in spite of the financial ruin that faced him as a result. All that remained for him was the late pope's cat, now the faithful companion of Chateaubriand's declining years.

IX *Aftermath of the July Revolution*

An even more extravagant gesture was to follow, when the revolution of July, 1830, forced the abdication of Charles X and put Louis-Philippe in his place; Chateaubriand resigned his membership in the House of Peers and refused to swear an oath of loyalty to the new king.

Meanwhile, the very long project of the "Complete Works," whose publication was begun in 1826, finally reached an end in 1831 with the *Historical Studies*, an unpublished work long promised but which Chateaubriand was only then able to complete. Once again, however, as a result of the publisher's bankruptcy, the financial rewards he had hoped for were not forthcoming; the painful money difficulties continued. This was after all not surprising—nothing seems to indicate that Chateaubriand was particularly frugal, and he admits that Mme de Chateaubriand liked to entertain in high style. Without a family fortune to back up this style of life, money problems were unavoidable.

Chateaubriand's later years, especially from the point of view of politics, can be appreciated only if we take into account a rather extraordinary woman, the duchess of Berry. She was, it will be remembered, the wife of one of the sons of Charles X. When the duke was assassinated at the Opera House, the duchess was expecting a child. According to some reports, antilegitimists tried all manner of means to cause a miscarriage, thus to extinguish the royal line; for example, explosions were said to have been set off outside the duches's windows. But the posthumous son was born, destined to become "Henry V" to the legitimists, who recognized him as king rather than Louis-Philippe.

In 1830, Charles X and his family had been banished. They went first to Scotland, then to Prague. But Mme de Berry was not satisfied to live in simple exile. To her supporters, including Chateaubriand, she was a heroic woman struggling to restore sanity to the French government; to her enemies, she was a simple intrigante, wreaking havoc wherever she went.

As one of her projects, Mme de Berry set up a "shadow cabinet" of people favorable to the legitimist cause. Chateaubriand was asked to join this secret cabinet. Meanwhile Mme de Berry landed in Provence with a small army, expecting to collect great numbers of supporters as she went, on the model of Napoleon on his return from Elba. However, she lacked Napoleon's magic, and the followers failed to appear; she was forced to fly to the province of Vendée, one of the royalist strongholds. For his supposed part in this venture, Chateaubriand was arrested and spent a short time in jail, then under house arrest. After two weeks, however, charges were dropped.

Chateaubriand decided this was a good time for a trip to Switzerland. Meanwhile, Mme de Berry was arrested and imprisoned in Bordeaux. Hearing once more the call of duty, Chateaubriand returned to Paris in 1832 to publish a pamphlet in defense of the duchess. For having made public his declaration to the duchess—"Madame, your son is my King"—he and the journals printing the remark were brought to trial. In the France of Louis-Philippe such a remark was sedition. Once again, the result was an acquittal, and Chateaubriand's statement became the rallying cry of the legitimists.

Still in prison, Mme de Berry smuggled a letter to Chateaubriand asking him to go to Prague. He was to carry two letters, one to the dauphine, Mme de Berry's sister-in-law, and one to Henry V. Both were written in lemon juice so the writing would be invisible until heated. The need for haste was occasioned by Mme de Berry's admission, perhaps under persuasion during her imprisonment, that she had married an Italian count. The public reaction to the case of a cherished public figure, recently widowed by the assassin's crime, marrying a foreigner, was much to be feared. This was especially so, since there was a duel between Mme de Berry's forces and those of Charles X over the control of Henry V's education, and adverse public opinion could well weaken Mme de Berry's position.

Chateaubriand of course accepted the task, but seems to have met with little success in his dealings with the French royal family in Bohemia. On his return, Mme de Berry had already been released and deported to Italy. She called him to Venice and planned a second trip which Chateaubriand took to Prague, this time involved with the question of Henry V and his reaching the majority. Again, the results were inconclusive. In October, 1833, Chateaubriand returned to Paris.

He still had fifteen years to live, but these years were not to see the great political activity of the earlier times. Nor was he to undertake any more extended travels. Both money and health were considerations. These last years were taken up in finishing and polishing the *Memoirs*. Theoretically, the *Memoirs* were finished in 1841, but subsequent events required a considerable amount of later revision. Another important literary occupation was *The Life of Rancé*, a work of penance undertaken at his confessor's suggestion. This biography, published in 1844, is in many ways one of the author's most intriguing books, and one of the literary summits of his career.

Mme de Chateaubriand died not long before Chateaubriand himself. The aged widower, approaching the end of his seventies, immediately offered his hand to Mme Récamier, as a last honorable gesture. She refused the offer. Not long after, on July 4, 1848, he died, following on yet another revolution, that of 1848, which allowed him to see how judicious he had been in doubting the stability of the July monarchy; had he lived a few years longer, he would have seen another of his theories proved: France was likewise not yet able to support a stable republic.

CHAPTER 2

Three Novellas
Atala, René, The Last Abencerraje

ALTHOUGH the chronology of publication dates separates the *Abencerraje* from the other two novellas, they nevertheless form an entity. Chateaubriand himself grouped them for publication in his *Complete Works,* and they resemble one another in length, manner, and subject. All three evoke, against a background of colorful scenes, the Romantic depiction of contraried love.

I Atala

Atala was certainly the best known of Chateaubriand's works during his lifetime. Critics today still respect the tale, giving it second place among the author's works after the *Memoirs.*

The particular form the story takes comes certainly from Chateaubriand's experience of America, not necessarily the actual America that he saw, but the imaginary America he created not only out of his travels but largely out of his readings. The fact must be borne in mind that he was not attempting an accurate realistic portrayal of early America. With an almost surrealist technique, although long before the time of the Surrealist school, Chateaubriand was attempting to paint a picture of America which, although entirely false in many of its details, would become more vivid, more real in the psychological sense than life itself.

A most apt comparison was made by the modern novelist Julien Gracq in speaking of *Atala.* He called Chateaubriand's work a painting which had the "inexhaustible charm of a Douanier Rousseau." The painter Rousseau is a good comparison. He was a primitive, and his paintings, many of which are jungle and animal scenes, are artificial and childlike in their simplicity. He is nonetheless a great painter who was able to seize the essential qualities of the scene he was painting and to transmit his own sensations to the beholder.

Chateaubriand did much the same thing. Although he peoples the banks of the Mississippi with blue herons, green flamingos, bears drunk from eating grapes, and although he mixes together the flora and fauna of the most disparate regions, he succeeds in presenting an incredibly vivid, almost psychedelic image of the wilderness.

The composition of *Atala* is also bound up with another of Chateaubriand's works, *The Genius of Christianity*. One of the theses of this book was the superiority of Christianity as a source of literary inspiration over the classical myths and episodes which were alone thought the proper subject matter for serious literature in the seventeenth, and even largely in the eighteenth, century. The tale of *Atala* was to serve as an illustration of these principles.

Chateaubriand says in *The Genius*:

In Christianity . . . religion and ethics are one and the same thing. The Scriptures enlighten us on our origin and instruct us concerning our own natures; the Christian mysteries concern us directly: we see ourselves everywhere therein; it was for us that the Son of God sacrificed Himself. From Moses to Jesus Christ, from the Apostles to the Church Fathers, everything offers the painting of the inner personality, everything tends to dissipate the darkness which covers it: and it is one of the distinctive characteristics of Christianity that it has always involved man with God, while the false religions have separated the Creator from the creature.

There is therefore an incalculable advantage in the Christian Religion, which the poets should have recognized, instead of having decried it obstinately. For not only is it just as beautiful as polytheism in the *marvellous,* or in the relationships among the elements of the *supernatural,* as we shall attempt to show hereafter, but also it has a dramatic and ethical dimension which polytheism did not have. (II, ii, 1.)

Atala is divided into three main parts, Prologue, The Tale, and Epilogue. The Tale is itself divided into subsections: "The Hunters," "The Tillers," "The Drama," and "The Funeral." After a long descriptive introduction, prized as one of the masterpieces of word painting in French, we meet the main character, Chactas, an old man at the time of the narration. But the main portion of the work embodies Chactas' retelling of his love for Atala.

It is René, the young Frenchman and hero of *René* and *The Natchez*, who is Chactas' audience.

The plot can be told very rapidly. Captured by an enemy tribe, Chactas is to be put to death. A maiden of the enemy tribe falls in love with Chactas, and together they escape. Wandering in the forest, they come upon a mission where the benefits of civilization are being taught the Indians. Chactas is sure his joy will be eternal. All hopes are dashed, however, when Atala takes poison. We learn that at Atala's birth, her mother, a Christian, had so feared for the child's life that she swore to the Queen of Angels an oath of virginity for Atala. This was the reason for the poison: Atala felt that if she married Chactas, her mother would be damned.

Atala dies and is buried in the Indian cemetery.

Chateaubriand takes the simple story of two young Indians of different tribes and also of different religions: Chactas remains faithful to the ancient Indian lore, while Atala is a convert to Christianity. Atala's mistaken belief in the immutability of her mother's vow of virginity for Atala precipitates the final suicide of the Indian girl in the arms of Chactas.

The author tells us that his original intention was to insert Atala into the pages of *The Genius*, as he did with the similar tale of *René*. However, *Atala* did in fact appear separately in 1801 while the text of *The Genius* was not to appear until 1802.

The precise motives for this early separate publication can be debated. Chateaubriand stated that he had read fragments of *Atala* in the various salons he frequented and that the work was attracting so much attention that he felt it necessary to publish it immediately, for fear of destroying the effect. However, one might also suspect that Chateaubriand was carefully preparing the way for the more extensive work he was undertaking by creating an advance interest which would arouse the impatience of the public anxious to read the entire text of *The Genius*. Such commercial and promotional considerations can be attributed to Chateaubriand without fear: the extraordinary "management" of the publication for his *Memoirs* gives ample evidence of his expertise in this domain.

For whatever motives, the work did appear in 1801. It created an immediate sensation. Chateaubriand was suddenly an overnight success. The book was devoured as it passed from hand to hand. Few works of lasting value have seen such immediate success. This extreme enthusiasm of the audience accounts for one of the reasons for studying *Atala* today; it is not the only reason, to be sure, because the esthetic considerations far outweigh the historical ones. But since these historical considerations are easier to deal with, they can be discussed first.

Atala is at the same time a perfect reflection of the tastes of the early nineteenth century and a powerful influence on the attitudes of generations to come. First of all, the tale is an exact representation of the remains of classical influence still exerting their pressure in the early 1800's. The language is ornamented and rhetorical; the phrases are ordered with perfect harmony and balance. Classical allusions abound. The language itself recalls classical texts in its phrasing. A kind of detached Olympian attitude coexists with the far different sentiments which can be identified as the beginnings of Romanticism.

This foundation of Classicism is everywhere present in Chateaubriand as it is in the early period. This classical foundation serves as the basis for the construction of a new kind of novel, a new literature. Instead of attempting to emphasize the universal elements in the manner of the Classicists, rather than attempting to discover what is the same in all men, Chateaubriand attempts to focus his attention on individuals. What interests him is not what makes his characters like all other men, but on the contrary, what makes them different.

The involvement is first of all on a sentimental level. We are not dealing in *Atala* with great universal passions as in the Classical tragedies. We are dealing with the specific emotions and feelings of clearly defined individuals. While the Classicist deals with the horror of an Oedipus, Chateaubriand deals with the melancholy of a Chactas.

This individualistic manner of painting characters and emotions extends to the settings. And in fact, the settings often take precedence over the other elements. Chateaubriand pushes the desire for specific setting to the point of choosing the landscape which will be the most unfamiliar to the reader, the American wilderness.[2] This exoticism of setting is one of the characteristics which can be found throughout the literature of the first half of the nineteenth century.

The influence of *Atala* is equally easy to define. Chateaubriand is frequently referred to by critics as "the revealer." What he revealed was America. For generations of Frenchmen, America

was the primitive and exotic painting Chateaubriand had prepared. The literary progeny of *Atala* are as numerous as they
are obscure today. It is possible to trace the story's influence
through all of Romantic literature, both in France and abroad,
and even to trace the negative influence of the work, that is
the reaction, among the Realists and later the Naturalists, against
such works as *Atala*.

The esthetic values of the novel are of course much more subtle
and therefore much more difficult to define. The first of these—
the question of style—is a value not limited to the work at hand,
but common to all of Chateaubriand's writings.[3] Chateaubriand
was for his contemporaries, and remains even today, a model
of beauty and elegance in style.

The esthetic value which is perhaps one limited to *Atala* alone
is the primitive painting of nature that has already been mentioned. In attempting to characterize this element, we need the
perspective of the 150 years which separate us from the work.
Atala is we see it is certainly different from the work that the
contemporaries saw. For them, if it was no doubt the best, it
was also only one of the Indian tales then current. For us,
there is an essential difference between *Atala* and the other works
of the period, an added dimension which has allowed it to
survive.

To resume the comparison of the primitive painting: the ad-
jective must be taken in its technical sense, that is as designating
a naïve and self-learned technique. The comparison must not
be pushed too far, as in matters of style Chateaubriand was the
most learned, the most academic artist conceivable. Yet in his
presentation of an extremely personal interpretation, he achieves
something which is psychologically infinitely more moving than
a straightforward "photographic" portrait.

A specific example may serve to illustrate this point. One of
the most moving scenes of the work is the death of Atala.
Chateaubriand sets out to create a sensation of overwhelming
beauty and pathos. Just as the ancients did not want to elicit
either pity or terror but rather both, Chateaubriand deems it
essential to combine his two elements. Taken on a realistic scale,
Chateaubriand's portrayal is ludicrous: his Indian girl has golden
hair and her skin is white as alabaster, so transparent that the pale
blue veins can be seen. Although the *Travels in America* are
largely fabrication and literary reminiscence, the author did

after all spend a certain time in America and did see authentic Indians. Therefore, he is distorting reality for a purpose—a purpose bound up with artistic motives.

This willful distortion of truth is perhaps not without precedent. The extent to which Prévost[4] was willful in his distortion is perhaps debatable, but there can be no question about the results. When he has his heroine die in the sandy deserts around New Orleans, he is obviously not dealing in realities. His scene required a vast expanse of nothingness for his characters. Manon Lescaut tramping through a bayou was not artistically conceivable. Perhaps Prévost was unaware of the features of the New Orleans area, but the fact remains that if he did not know the nature of the terrain, he took no steps to ascertain the reality: it was not important for his purposes.

In this same way, Chateaubriand willfully puts aside his authentic recollections and draws a portrait that will have great intrinsic plastic beauty. The subject must be beautiful as well as the portrayal. Chateaubriand did not seek to ally pathos with ugliness or with strangeness, but with beauty in a very classical sense: the beauty of a Greek statue. Only by making this combination could he achieve his end. The author is in effect asking the reader to suspend his judgment, his knowledge (if any) of the reality which stands behind his portrayal, and to conceive of the work of art simply as a vehicle for transmitting an impression, a view of a superior reality.

This does not mean that everything in *Atala* is necessarily an exaggeration or a transposition. For example, one of the greatest values in *Atala* is to be found in the vast poetic descriptions of nature that abound in the work. They exist apart from the rest of the work almost as if they were poems. Indeed, good arguments can be offered proving that Chateaubriand was one of the earliest of prose poets.[5] When we see a sunset as described by Chateaubriand, it is perhaps raised to the level of perfection seldom reached in nature, but all the elements of the description are completely authentic.

Such is not the case, however, with the other elements of the work. There is, for example, a profusion of color, an agglutination of fragments of picturesque detail which actually clash with one another, but which serve to stimulate the imagination in the most effective way.

It is above all this stimulation to the imagination which makes the greatness of Chateaubriand's evocations. Almost to the extent of affecting the reactions of a taker of drugs, Chateaubriand paints a mental picture that can be astonishing. Thus is created a surprising combination of traditional beauty and strikingly new beauty that parallels the subject-matter combination of classical traditional form and innovative sentiments. Side by side exist the beauties of a typical plastic nature, as for example in Atala's death scene, and some of the wildest and most imaginative effects of color and light, as seen for example in the description of the banks of the Mississippi.

II   René

René is in many ways as closely tied to The Genius of Christianity as Atala, perhaps even more closely since it did in fact appear as a part of that larger work as originally planned; it was not to be published by itself until three years later. But in a certain sense the attachment is artificial. To be sure, the chapter of The Genius entitled "On the Vagueness of the Passions" exposes the theory upon which René is edified. One may be permitted to ask, however, whether this chapter is truly an integral part of the work, or whether it is one of those more or less artificial transitions Chateaubriand sometimes indulges in.

Whatever the case, the chapter explains the phenomenon to be painted in the story: what was to be called by later authors the mal du siècle, the disease of the century. These later authors were to find a multiplicity of explanations for the "disease," explanations from the domain of history and sociology. For Chateaubriand, however, it is a combination of mental and physiological states. At that point in which the desires and the passions of the individual have developed, but before these passions can be satisfied, there occurs this intermediate and confused state in which the individual does not know himself, cannot analyze his sentiments, cannot bring any remedy to his melancholy—all this for no reason that he can fathom.

It is clear in Chateaubriand's explanatory passages that this is a temporary phase. It is a disease of adolescence which will pass with the years. This is why, in the final pages of the story, we find the missionary, Father Souël, attempting to advise and counsel the young man in this very way:

"Nothing," he said to the brother of Amélie, "nothing in this story merits the pity you have been shown here. I see a young man filled with chimaeras, who dislikes everything, and who has withdrawn from the burdens of society to indulge himself in useless reveries. One is not a superior being, sir, because one finds the world hateful. One does not hate men and life except for lack of perspective. Look a bit further, and you will soon be convinced that all these ills you complain of are non-existent. . . . What are you doing alone in the depths of the forests where you live out your life, neglecting all your duties? You tell me that saints have hidden themselves in forests. They were there with their tears, spending their days attempting to extinguish their passions, while you perhaps spend your time feeding yours."

Chateaubriand is careful not to show us the cure, however. Whatever the author's "scientific" pretensions might be, he is always first and foremost an artist. The would-be scientist will not be allowed to spoil the artistic portrait of René by "curing" him. A normal René would have lost all the charm of the melancholy René.

The year 1802, then, marked the publication of *René* together with *The Genius of Christianity*. Its esthetic interest, however, goes far beyond the parent work, as does *Atala*. This story complements the earlier tale in its portrait of the early nineteenth-century psyche: *Atala* portrayed the exotic colors of nature and the strangeness of foreign places and individuals; *René* paints the tortures, self-inflicted, of course, of the individual hero whose concept of destiny is that of a capricious fate which blows him about as if he were a dead leaf.

René is an adolescent who lives in a feudal castle very reminiscent of the Chateaubriand castle at Combourg. The young man has a sister, Amélie, who resembles enormously Chateaubriand's sister Lucile. As with *Atala*, the plot can be summarized in a few lines: Amélie realizes she bears an incestuous love for her brother; she retires to a convent and René flees to America to attempt to forget his melancholy. It is in the country of the Natchez that he tells his sad tale to Chactas, who is now an old man.

Such a subject has of course been a field day for the biographical critics. Such an incestuous love, according to them, obviously reflects a similarly incestuous love of Chateaubriand's sister Lucile for the author. Modern critics would simply dismiss the question as of no importance: the artistic creation is a thing apart from the life of the creator. This problem need not be dismissed without proof, however. The fact is that the theme of incestuous love was a very popular one in late eighteenth-century literature. It so happens that the outstanding masterpiece utilizing this subject is *René*, but this should not obscure the fact that countless other novels were based on the same materials. Chateaubriand is merely exploiting an already discovered mine. The ways in which these materials suited Chateaubriand's purpose will be seen in a moment.

The exotic element does play a role in *René* as in *Atala*, since the melancholy youth travels to America, making use of the classic panacea for melancholy, travel (but of course it does not work, as it never does). However, the interest in *René* is to a far greater extent a psychological one rather than a pictorial one: it is the study of René's unhappiness that fills the center of the stage.

And yet, this is not entirely true. Chateaubriand is always far too complex to be explained in a single phrase. An important exception must be made so far as the pictorial element is concerned, as regards religion. We return here again to the ground of *The Genius*, and it is perhaps here that *René* truly fits into the scheme of the larger work. Over and over again, Chateaubriand states that religion is a powerful source of literary inspiration. The early-nineteenth-century readers and authors are above all visually and sentimentally oriented. The abstract awe and majesty of the religious dogmas are not the element in religion which most attracts the individual of this type. In religion, he seeks what is picturesque and what will appeal most immediately to the emotions. Instead of the distance and perspective that the classical authors sought, Chateaubriand wants an immediacy which causes a strong emotional reaction without need for reflection.

A good example is perhaps the liturgical incense. The smoke rising from the burning incense is an idea which as a symbol would have greatly affected an earlier, or a later, audience: as the smoke rises to heaven, so the prayers rise up to God. But for Chateaubriand, the incense is first of all a pleasant smell, something to create a favorable reaction without the need for analysis. Second, the smell of the incense in its associations with the whole religious experience, is capable of bypassing the other and more substantial elements of the experience, so that an entire climate of events can be re-created through the associations bound up in only one of its elements: in short, what one might call today a "Proustian experience."

It is because of the need for these visual and physical stimuli that we find in *René* (and here again, Chateaubriand is typical of his age) constant and detailed descriptions of the details of religious ceremonies. The literature of the times was to become laden down with often gratuitous and seemingly endless descriptions of marriages, baptisms, funerals, masses, and the like. Chateaubriand uses these same techniques, but with discretion, and it is in his discretion that a great deal of his art lies.

The circumstance of the incestuous love and the need to find a haven where Amélie will be protected from her passions form the extremely useful justification for the religious descriptions, extremely useful since this serves as a stimulus to the evocation of the whole spectrum of religious or pseudo-religious experience; and indeed if the experience is left at the level of the visual and physical elements, it can be finally only a pseudo-religious experience. Parenthetically it must be noted, however, that the mystical religious experience is not typical of French literature or even of French religious thought. In fact, in France the mystics were more often than not thought to be considered religiously unsound or even dangerously heretical. One needs cite only the examples of Pascal and Mme Guyon's Quietist movement.

We thus find long passages devoted to the convent, to the nuns, and to the actual ceremony of the taking of the veil, complete with the obligatory swoon. One can feel that Chateaubriand is thrilled by this religious spectacle, and in turn the emotion is communicated to the reader, whatever his convictions and however blasé he may consider himself.

Once this very important visual element is dealt with, however, we must return to the central question of the psychological portrait of the hero. "Psychological" is perhaps not a word often applied to Chateaubriand's portraits, but this may be unjustified. We are conditioned to think of psychology as being a characteristic of Stendhal in his writings, or of Racine. In each case, there is a cool and calculating analysis on the part of the author, an analysis which is presented by an individual who stands apart and views his characters with the cold, calculating eye of an anatomist about to start dissecting. Chateaubriand, on the other hand, presents us with an effusion of emotion which by its very exaggeration makes us consider it unrealistic and therefore unscientific as a psychological analysis. As a matter of fact, there is some of the Racinian or Stendhalian analysis in the words of Father Souël already referred to, but the truly great insight comes rather in another way out of the very extravagances of René.

When one is attempting to assess the greatness of Molière's comedies, it is generally a question of extracting his characters from their times and attempting to equate their foibles with those of the man of today. Molière stands up admirably to this dislocation in time: he was a master at seeking out and identifying all the weaknesses of man, weaknesses which were not the result of the times but the result of human nature.

Will Chateaubriand stand such dislocation in time? A careful examination of the character of René must give an affirmative answer. Various times and various circumstances give different outlets to the feelings that Chateaubriand paints, but the misery, the frustration, the desperate search for solidity, stability, constant values, understanding—all these things are characteristic of human nature as Chateaubriand saw it and as it exists today. The same eternal problems with the same apparent impossibility of resolution give proof of Chateaubriand's truly visionary grasp of the adolescent soul. It is for this reason that René, in spite of the vast changes in the outward manifestations of society since the time of Chateaubriand, remains a remarkable assessment of the functioning of the human mind and its tangled maze of sentiments, which by their very lack of logic lend themselves not to the cold and calculating scientific anaylsis but rather to the unbridled outpouring of emotion that we see in René.

III   The Last Abencerraje[6]

In many ways, *The Last Abencerraje* is the most personal of Chateaubriand's works, second only to the *Memoirs*. Just as the *Memoirs* were a kind of secret document, not to be published until after the author's death, this short novel had to wait many years until it was revealed to the general public. It is true that the work was read from time to time in various salons and groups, but always to a select coterie of friends and acquaintances.

Therefore it was not until 1826 that *The Last Abencerraje* finally appeared, grouped with *Atala and René* in the Ladvocat collection of Chateaubriand's complete works. The story had remained unpublished since its composition in 1808-9.

Moreover, it was not for lack of interest that the work was not printed. Because of the personal nature of the work, the history of composition and publication has been minutely studied. There is ample evidence of several occasions in the years between 1809 and 1826 when Chateaubriand was on the point of publishing, but always against his will. Generally, it was a question of dire financial necessity, although there were also certain political questions: during Napoleon's difficulties in his subjugation of Spain, Chateaubriand's open defense of the Spanish national character could have caused grave problems for an author who had so publicly indicated his opposition to Napoleon.

Each time he considered publishing it, however, loans from friends and prudence caused Chateaubriand to replace the manuscript in its folder, keeping it once again from the public. Why this excessive hesitation to display a work which he obviously considered one of his best? It is because the story had a double set of sources, as is so regularly the case with Chateaubriand, literary sources and personal sources. In this case, the personal sources are so closely attached to his private life that publication would seem to be a desecration, especially with the tragic fate of the lady who inspired the character of Blanca.

This lady was Natalie de Noailles. Chateaubriand met her shortly before he was to embark on his trip to Jerusalem to seek inspiration for the epic he wished to compose and which appeared as *The Martyrs*. From this trip was also to come a travel book, the *Itinerary from Paris to Jerusalem*. The couple felt an immediate attraction. Natalie de Noailles did not seek to dissuade him from his trip, however: she recognized the importance of it for the future literary reputation of the author.

He planned to visit the eastern Mediterranean first, returning through Spain. They arranged to meet there on Chateaubriand's return. The romantic associations with the already romantic Spanish milieu inspired the tale Chateaubriand was to compose. The situation was one particularly appropriate to a person of Chateaubriand's turn of mind: a kind of "love at first sight" followed by a long separation in which the object of the author's affections can in his imagination take on the aura of idealization.

For someone who lived much more by imagination than by fact, the importance of this idealization is obvious. It has been said by Chateaubriand's intimates that Natalie de Noailles was the only woman he ever truly loved. This is perhaps true, but it is an open question whether it was Natalie the reality or Natalie the myth whom Chateaubriand really loved.

The liaison continued throughout the trip from Madrid to France, and Chateaubriand remained her ardent admirer in Paris until the day of a falling-out, which appears to have been a rejection on the part of Natalie since Chateaubriand continued in his fervent admiration. The end of Natalie is a sad one. She fell prey to a mental disorder, completely losing her mind.

So it was that only when these events were far in the past did Chateaubriand feel able to publish the work. In composing it, he obviously pictured himself, tanned by exposure to the elements in the Near East, as the young Arab coming from Africa to Spain, where he meets the beautiful European. Once again, however, the works of Chateaubriand must not be read as an autobiography. The same care that must be used in approaching *René* must be used here, because we are not dealing with facts but with the literary transposition of a set of idealized circumstances.

The Last Abencerraje is at first very different from *Atala* and *René*. The locale, the actors, the plot, everything is different. At the same time, this short novel represents just as precisely as the first two the literary currents of the beginnings of Romanticism. Here as before, Chateaubriand does not differ markedly from his contemporaries; he is not a startling innovator. His merit lies in the fact that he is the most complete and, more important, the most artistically perfect representation of his age.

Thus, as *Atala* followed in the wake of a series of Indian novels, as *René* imitated the current of sentimental reverie, the *Abencerraje* retraced the footsteps of a legion of Spanish and especially Mauresque tales. Once again, however, the forerunners are completely forgotten today. The *Abencerraje* remains as a literary monument.

In the style of many of the earlier novels, the *Abencerraje* contains several poems, romances sung by the various characters. Two of these are interesting since they are based on authentic Spanish *romances* which were only beginning to be translated and appreciated in France as a genre. The third is the most

celebrated piece of poetry written by Chateaubriand—"I have
a fond memory . . ."—which he had composed earlier but which
he inserted in the *Abencerraje*.

As is so often the case with Chateaubriand, the plot is an
exceedingly simple one. The two central characters are Blanca,
a Spanish girl of noble family, and Aben-Hamet, the last survivor
of the famed Moorish race of the Abencerrajes. It is some time
after the *Reconquista,* the date (1492) that marked the final
defeat of the infidels by the Spanish on the European Continent.
A few Moors remain in Spain, having adopted Christianity, but
for the most part they have fled to North Africa. Charles V now
rules in Spain and Francis I in France.

With a secret purpose in mind, Aben-Hamet sets out to visit
Granada, the home of his ancestors. On arriving, he meets and
immediately falls in love with Blanca. She in turn loves him,
and her father is greatly impressed by the young Moor. All that
stands between them is religion. "Become a Christian and I
shall be yours," says Blanca. "Become a Muslim and you will
be my Sultana," says Aben-Hamet. Both remain unswerving in
their loyalties. Aben-Hamet is called home by the death of his
mother, but the lovers arrange to meet in a year. After the year's
end, Aben-Hamet returns; both have remained faithful to one
another, but they remain equally faithful to their respective
religions. They part, and once again meet at the end of a year.
The situation is unchanged. This time, however, Aben-Hamet
meets Blanca's brother, who takes an immediate dislike to him,
because he wants his sister to marry a friend of his, a French
knight. He orders Aben-Hamet to leave, and when he refuses,
the brother insists on a duel. Aben-Hamet is the victor, but
spares his adversary's life.

It is now that Aben-Hamet discovers that Blanca and her
brother are the last descendants of the Spanish national hero,
the Cid. The reader now learns the secret purpose that first
brought Aben-Hamet to Spain: to seek out the descendants of
the Cid. He wishes to avenge the wrongs the Cid caused his
ancestors. But he has become too involved to wreak his vengeance.
In a quandary, he asks Blanca what to do. Barely able to speak
because of emotion, she says: "Return to the desert." He does
this, and the lovers remain forever separated.

Chateaubriand is again dealing with the subject matter he
likes best: an impossible love intertwined with religion. In *Atala,*

it was the mother's vow which separated the lovers; in *René*, the shadow of incest makes love impossible. Here it is the conflicting religions which separate the two.

It is curious to see how Chateaubriand handles these problems of religion. In *The Genius of Christianity* he had attempted to show the natural superiority of Christianity over all other religions, and indeed in the *Abencerraje* he has Aben-Hamet come very close to being converted when he enters a Christian church. However, the religious separation is underscored by the antagonism of the nationalities and by the personal antagonisms of the two races of heroes, so that a reconciliation becomes impossible.

The novel is consciously archaic. From the point of view of manner and technique, it is very close to the seventeenth- and eighteenth-century models the author has in mind. The associations with Corneille's play of the *Cid* (as with other seventeenth-century plays) and with the works of the greatest of seventeenth-century novelists, Mme de La Fayette, are more than obvious. Near-quotations and references abound. The result is that, as with Mme de La Fayette's *The Princess of Clèves*, *The Abencerraje* is a model of the concise analytical novel of hopeless love.

There is, however, another dimension to the novel which belongs more to the times of the author: the setting. Relatively little description of scenes is to be found in the earlier novels of Moorish Spain. Here, however, the settings become one of the most important elements and one of the principal merits of the work. In particular, the description of the Alhambra by moonlight as visited by the two lovers forms one of the most successful evocations of all French literature.

In an attempt to assess the over-all value of the work, it will be perhaps useful to return for a moment to the personal life of the author. The question of Natalie de Noailles's role in the genesis of the work has been alluded to above. For almost a hundred years after the publication of the work, critics were convinced that this was an idealized transposition of the actual meeting of René and Natalie in the gardens of the Alhambra. Relatively recently, some began to doubt this and attempted to prove that Chateaubriand saw Granada alone and did not meet Natalie until afterward. The resulting controversy raged (the word is none too strong) for years. Even after the introduction of the most convincing evidence, readers refused to be won over.

This is perhaps the best possible tribute to the author. He has transmitted such a vision of reality and actuality that the reader can only comprehend it as the most personal of revelations.[7]

In truth, as is so typical of Chateaubriand the artist, the case was this: Chateaubriand rather rapidly saw the sights of Granada. His artist's eye was capable of gaining a general impression which went straight to the heart of the subject. Later, the literary associations—the accounts of other authors—come to attach themselves to this impression. Together with the transposed feelings for Natalie, he welds them into a cohesive whole, whose constituent parts are visible only as the result of patient scholarship.

From all points of view, for exotic description, for character analysis, and for beauty of expression, *The Last Abencerraje* certainly ranks with the masterpieces of Chateaubriand.

CHAPTER 3

The Religious Revival:
The Genius of Christianity

THE *Genius of Christianity* is an extremely difficult book with which to deal; yet it is an essential work not only for Chateaubriand but for the entire school of Romantic literature. It is perhaps because of the fact that the work is so inextricably bound up with its times that it becomes difficult to analyze. It is so diffuse, it covers such a vast area, that a tightly-knit construction and logical development from point to point are impossible.

In a very general way, the subject of the book is Christianity from the Romanticist's point of view: the emotions, the associations, and the inspirations to be derived from religion particularly in its application to the individual sensitivities and their reflection in literature.

I *Background of the Revival*

Some background is necessary. Under the *ancien régime* France took great pride in being the "eldest daughter of the Church." But the eighteenth-century *philosophes* and the later revolutionaries saw in religion something undeniably and irrevocably linked with the old monarchy. They considered the church and the government equally corrupt. Therefore, when the time came to overthrow one, the other had necessarily to be overthrown in like manner. In a situation which has its parallels in modern times, religion was outlawed, the churches were closed, and clerics and religious forced into the world and denied the practice of their functions.

But again, as has been seen in modern times, religion cannot be abolished by fiat. In turn-of-the-century France there was a combination of moral and political need for the re-establishment of religion. A kind of "religious underground" had de-

58

veloped with priests saying mass first in secret and then more and more openly. The revolutionary substitutes for religion, the establishment of a goddess of reason and the like, had failed miserably. At the same time, Napoleon as ruler of France was finding political difficulties in the situation: the "underground" priests were in secret communication with their émigré bishops who had fled France with the nobles. This represented then a distinct danger to Napoleon's government: a royalist counter-revolution which might erupt at any moment.

Napoleon understandably took action, culminating in the Concordat with the pope in 1801 whereby Catholicism was re-established in France. This allowed the creation of a new church hierarchy, loyal to Napoleon instead of to the king, on the model of the empire nobility that Napoleon was to institute in his court, thus assuring himself of solid support on both sides.

It was at this incredibly propitious moment that Chateaubriand's work appeared on the scene (1802). Those wishing to magnify Chateaubriand's role credit him with sparking a veritable renaissance of religious fervor. Those wishing to disparage him paint the author as a materialistic opportunist grasping at the popular subject of the day. The truth lies between the two extremes. Chateaubriand both represented the thinking of his epoch and influenced it. It would be vain to attempt to determine exactly what the proportions were: the best course of action is to recognize the fact of this double nature of the influences—on Chateaubriand and from Chateaubriand.

Up to the nineteenth century, the basis of literary inspiration had been the classics. Greek and Roman literature afforded the models which the French writers attempted to emulate. Even when dealing with other subjects the form was classical: Voltaire in his *Henriade,* an epic poem of the times of the great Henry IV, modeled the work on the *Aeneid.* It is true one can point to exceptions: Racine chose to write a tragedy based on biblical history, *Athaliah,* but works of this kind remain exceptions. It is also true, to be sure, that in the course of the eighteenth century many authors experimented with nonclassical subject matter.

But the great resource of the Christian religion as literary inspiration remained untapped. This then is the message of the *Genius*: the elements of Christianity are just as capable of serving as stimulus to literary activity as the classics. But they have an advantage over the classics of being based not on legend and fantasy but on revealed truth.[1]

In the detail, however, Chateaubriand takes up the most disparate elements, showing everywhere the evocative power of suggestion: each element suggests a sentiment, creates a feeling. Many years later when Baudelaire wrote his poem, "Correspondances," he presented what is essentially the same idea, and even then it was still a new concept.[2] Chateaubriand in 1802 was already preaching the gospel of the power of the association of ideas.

II *Visual Elements of Religion*

The only way to grasp the scope of the work is to examine a few passages in detail, each one dealing with a different aspect of the text. A first example we may choose deals with the church sacraments, where Chateaubriand underscores the associations between modern baptism and the original biblical baptisms.

On the Sacraments
Baptism and Confession

See the neophyte standing in the waters of the Jordan: the hermit of the rock is pouring the lustral waters upon his head; the river of the patriarchs, the camels on the banks, the temple of Jerusalem, the cedars of Lebanon seem attentive; or rather look at the infant on the sacred fountain. A family of joy surrounds him; for him they renounce sin, they give him the name of his grandfather, who becomes immortal by this rebirth which love effects from line to line. Already the father hastens to take back his son, to carry him back to an impatient wife, who behind her bed-curtains is counting the strokes of the baptismal bell. They surround the mother's bed: tears of tenderness and religion flow from all eyes; the new name of the child, the old name of his ancestor, is repeated from mouth to mouth; each individual, combining the remembrance of things past with the present joys, seems to recognize the old man in the newborn who reawakens his memory. Such are the scenes which the sacrament of baptism presents; but religion, always ethical, always serious, even when it is most smiling, shows us also the son of kings in his purple renouncing the grandeur of Satan, at the same font where the child of the poor comes in rags to abjure the pomp to which however he will never be condemned. (I, i, 6)[3]

Chateaubriand's attitude in his examination of the sacraments and the church liturgy is always a pictorial one. He invariably

presents a scene full of color and character. But he does not stop
there. The picture must tell a story. It must be possible to sense
the motives, the feelings, the actions. One is inevitably drawn to
make the comparison with some of the eighteenth-century painters
such as Hogarth and Greuze whose paintings are designed to
tell a story. It is particularly interesting to compare Diderot's
art criticism with Chateaubriand. Diderot looks at a picture of
Greuze, for example, and puts down on paper the whole story
of the episode as he has deduced it from the painting.

If one is to apply here also the idea of *correspondances,* it is
obvious that what Chateaubriand does is to evoke an action,
baptism, which immediately conjures up the multiple associations
inextricably bound up with the action. The action thus gains an
added dimension which increases immeasurably the effect of
the scene on the sensitivities of the spectator or the reader. Above
all, it is important to realize that the liturgical elements are not
considered by Chateaubriand on an intellectual level. It is
rather the psychological and sentimental reaction that the elements provoke which interests the author.

Since these ceremonies, surrounded by scenes of richness and
pomp, are things of beauty in themselves, it is logical to find
that Chateaubriand and the other authors devote more and more
of their literary works to sometimes gratuitous depiction of the
liturgy and the sacraments. An excellent example in Chateaubriand is the scene in which René's sister Amélie becomes a nun
in an attempt to escape her incestuous love. This overpowering
and almost sensuous aura of religion permeates the literary works
of the entire period. Half a century later, Flaubert in his story
"A Simple Heart" painted a character, Félicité, who still saw
religion only from this pictorial and sensuous point of view. Her
delight at watching the communion ceremony, her need for
visualizing the Holy Ghost as a stuffed parrot, are the absurd
and extreme development of the attitudes of Chateaubriand's
era. Even Madame Bovary resembles this attitude: as a child
she invented sins to confess because she felt such sensual pleasure in going to confession.

As in so many other respects, then, Chateaubriand is here
at once the faithful representative of the attitudes of his times
and a striking innovator exercising great influence over his literary
contemporaries and followers.

III *Providence*

A second example of the materials used by Chateaubriand is to be found in the discussions of the existence of God.

*The Existence of God Proved by the Marvels of Nature
Songs of the Birds*

When the first silences of the night and the last murmurs of the day vie with one another on the hillsides, on the river banks, in the woods and the valleys; when the forests gradually become silent, when there is left not a single sigh from a leaf or a bit of moss, when the moon is in the heavens and the ear of man is attentive, the first chorister of the universe intones his hymns to the Eternal. First he strikes up the echo with brilliant sparks of pleasure: there is disorder in his songs; he jumps from low tones to high, from soft to loud; he pauses; he sings slowly, he sings rapidly: his is a heart intoxicated with joy, a heart palpitating under the burden of love. But suddenly the voice falls, the bird is silent. He begins again! How his tones have changed! What tender melody! At times there are languishing but varied modulations; at times there is a somewhat monotonous air, something like the old French ballads, masterpieces of simplicity and melancholy. The song is as often the mark of sadness as of joy: the bird which has lost its young still sings; it still repeats the air of happy times, for that is all it knows; but by a manipulation of its art, the musician needs change only his key, and the cantata of pleasure has become the lament of grief.

Those who seek to disinherit man, to take the empire of nature away from him, would like to prove that nothing is made particularly for us. But the song of the birds, for example, is so tailored to our ear that even though we persecute the guests of the forest, rob their nests, pursue them, wound them with arms or in traps, although we fill them with grief, we can not force them into silence. In spite of ourselves, they must charm us, they must accomplish the orders of Providence. . . .

The bird seems to be the veritable symbol of the Christian on the earth: he prefers, as do the faithful, solitude to society, the heavens to the earth; and his voice endlessly praises the Creator. (I, v, 5)

The question of providence was hotly discussed throughout the eighteenth century. The twentieth-century student however frequently has a distorted view of the controversy because the authors who are read today are the *philosophes* who denied the role of providence and made fun of the concept. In *Candide,* Voltaire has the character Pangloss declare that providence created noses so that man would have a place to rest his eyeglesses. But half a century later, Chateaubriand was still indulging in the same type of thinking that Voltaire was attempting to destroy in his satire. The important fact is that Voltaire's satire did not destroy the idea of providence, and, especially with the young royalist Romantics of the beginning of the nineteenth century, man still held the center of the universe: everything in the world had a purpose, and this purpose was bound up with the good of man.

But beyond the idea of the role of providence, this passage illustrates the point to which nature, just as religion, is a never-ending source of inspiration. Everything that is about him serves to intensify the individual's sensations. Once again, association of ideas and dramatization of the scene play an important role. Visual beauty combines with the mental beauties created by the association to explain the enormous attraction which nature in all its manifestations still holds for the Romantic author.

Once again, this attitude becomes a part of the literary scene to the extent that descriptions of nature, landscapes, animals, and flowers assume an important function in any work of art.

It is not necessary to go outside the *Genius* to find examples of Chateaubriand's precepts put into action. The author frequently stops and provides a sample which is often a masterpiece in its own right. Such a one is the following passage which exemplifies the power for beauty which Chateaubriand finds in nature.

The Existence of God Proved by the Marvels of Nature
Two Perspectives of Nature

What we have just said of animals and plants leads us to a consideration of the scenes of nature in a more general context. Let us try to make these things which separately have already told us so much about Providence speak together with one voice.

We shall present the reader with two perspectives of nature, one marine, the other terrestrial; one in the middle of the Atlantic; the other in the forests of the New World, so that the majesty of these scenes cannot be attributed to monuments constructed by man.

When the vessel on which we were passing over to America had gone beyond sight of land, all space was painted only with the double azure of sea and sky, like a canvas prepared for the future creations of some painter. The color of the waters became like that of liquid glass. A heavy sea was coming from the west, although the wind was blowing from the east; enormous swells extended from north to south, and in their valleys vistas of the vast emptiness of the ocean opened up. These moving landscapes changed their appearance at every moment: at times a multitude of green hillocks portrayed the rows of tombs in an immense cemetery; at times the waves, breaking into whitecaps, imitated white flocks spread through the heather. Often space seemed limited for lack of point of comparison. But if a wave rose up, a swell sloped down like a distant hill, a school of dogfish passed on the horizon, space suddenly opened up before us. There was above all the idea of great distance, when a slight mist was crawling along the surface of the sea, and seemed to make it even more immense. Oh, how the sight of the ocean is great and sad then! What reveries it plunges you into, whether the imagination dives into the Northern seas in the midst of hoar-frost and storms, or sails through the Southern seas to the isles of repose and happiness!

We would often get up in the middle of the night, and go to sit on the deck, where we would find only the officer on watch, and a few sailors smoking their pipes in silence. The only noise to be heard was the rustling of the prow on the waves, while burning sparks and white froth flew along the sides of the ship. God of the Christians! It is above all in the waters of the abyss and the depths of the skies that Thou hast graven the lines of Thy omnipotence! Millions of stars shining out of the sombre azure of the celestial dome, the moon in the center of the firmamant, a sea without shores, the infinite in the heaven and on the waters! Thou hast never more troubled me with Thy greatness than during those nights when suspended between the stars and the ocean, I had immensity over my head and immensity beneath my feet!

I am nothing; I am only a simple and solitary person; I have often heard the scholars arguing over the prime Being, and I have not understood them: but I have always noted that it is in the sight of the great scenes of nature that this unknown Being manifests Himself to the heart of man. One evening, (there was a dead calm), we found ourselves in those beautiful waters which bathe the shores of Virginia: all the sails were furled: I was busy below decks when I heard the bell which called the crew to prayer; I hastened to go and add my devotions to those of my traveling companions. The officers were on the poop deck with the passengers; the chaplain, a book in his hand, stood somewhat in front of them and the sailors were scattered helter-skelter over the main deck: we all stood facing the prow of the vessel to the west.

The sun's globe, ready to dip into the waters, could be seen through the ship's rigging in the midst of endless space. From the movement of the poop, the luminary appeared to change from horizon to horizon. A few clouds were strewn across the East, where the moon was rising slowly; the rest of the sky was pure; to the north, forming a glorious triangle with the luminary of day and that of the night, a waterspout brilliant with all the colors of the prism rose from the sea like a pillar of crystal supporting the vault of the heavens.

Anyone is to be pitied who could not recognize the beauty of God in this spectacle. In spite of myself, tears streamed from my eyes, when my companions, taking off their tarred hats intoned with a coarse voice the simple canticle to Our Lady of Perpetual Help, patroness of seafarers. How touching was the prayer of these men who on a fragile bit of wood in the middle of the ocean were contemplating the setting of the sun on the waters! How it penetrated straight to the soul, this invocation of the poor sailor to the Mater Dolorosa! The knowledge of our smallness in the sight of infinity, the sound of our songs extending out over the waves, the approach of the night with its pitfalls, the marvel of our vessel in the midst of so many marvels, a religious crew imbued with admiration and fear, an august priest in prayer, God leaning out over the abyss, with one hand holding back the sun at the gates of the occident and with the other lifting the moon in the east, and lending an attentive ear to the voice of His creature across the immensity: that is what could not possibly be painted and what the heart of man alone sufficed to feel.

Let us pass on to the terrestrial scene.

One evening I had wandered off in a forest at some distance from Niagara Falls; soon I saw light surrounding me, and I tasted, in all its solitude, the beautiful spectacle of the wilderness of the New World.

An hour after sunset, the moon appeared above the trees on the opposite horizon. A balsamed breeze which this queen of the night brought with her from the east, seemed to precede her in the forests like her cool breath. The lonely luminary rose little by little in the sky: at times it followed its azure course in a peaceful manner; at times it rested on groups of clouds which resembled the summits of high snow-covered mountains. These clouds, folding and unfolding their veils, unrolled to create diaphanous zones of white satin, dispersed in light flakes of foam, or formed banks of blinding cotton wool in the sky, so soft to the eye that one would seem to feel their elasticity.

The scene on the earth was no less delightful: the bluish velvety light of the moon filtered down through the spaces between the trees, and thrust sheaves of light even into the most remote darkness. The river flowing at my feet in turn lost itself in the woods and reappeared brilliant from the constellations of the night which it mirrored in its breast. In a savanna on the other side of the river the brilliance of

the moonlight slept motionless on the grass: birches in their clumps
here and there, rustled by the breeze, made islands of floating shadows
on this motionless sea of light. All about, everything would have been
silence and reprose except for the falling of a few leaves, the passing
of a gust of wind, the groaning of a screech owl; in the distance from
time to time could be heard the dull roar of Niagara Falls which
extended its sound through the wilderness to die in the solitary
forests.

The grandeur, the astonishing melancholy of this scene could not
possibly be expressed in human language; the most beautiful nights
in Europe cannot give the slightest idea of it. In vain in our cultivated
fields does the imagination seek to expand itself; everywhere it meets
with the dwelling places of man: but in these wild regions, the soul
is pleased to plunge into an ocean of forests, to glide over the gulf of
the cataracts, to meditate on the shores of the lakes and rivers, and
so to speak, to be alone before God. (I, v, 12)

The above passage is long, but it is worth quoting *in extenso*
because it is such a capital text from the point of view of both
stylistics and content. We shall return to the question of stylistics
and shall then examine this and other passages from that point
of view. But for the moment, let us examine the thought.

Here Chateaubriand's thesis of God manifesting Himself by
the grandeur of His creations is obvious. It is perhaps worth
noting that although Chateaubriand emphasizes the fact that
the beauty of the seascape and the landscape comes from the
solitude and absence of all traces of man, he repeatedly finds it
necessary to explain the scenes in terms of allusions to the pro-
ductions of man: the sky is a vault; the waterspout is a pillar;
the scene is like an artist's canvas.

Many pages could be written concerning the place of this passage in the history of French thought. There are obvious references to Pascal, who in his *Thoughts* dwelt at length on what he
described as the two infinites of greatness and smallness and the
insignificance of man.

But Chateaubriand, in tune with his century, considers religion
something which is felt, not discussed. At the sight of the marvelous spectacle of nature which he witnesses, he is filled with
emotion which is suggested to him by the obvious associations
and by the solemnity of the occasion, which gives rise to the
religious exclamations.

The frequent insistence of Chateaubriand on the impossibility of describing such scenes is another factor to be noted. Obviously, he does not take this too seriously, as he has just finished trying to describe the landscape and the seascape. But the picture must be, or must appear to be, beyond human understanding, and certainly the phenomenon must be beyond the capacity of any human to imitate, just as the individual cannot approach God through any process of reasoning and calculation, but must feel His presence as it permeates the universe.

IV *Role of Passion*

Book II of the second part is entitled: "Poetry in its relationship to man: Characters." The third book bears the same title except instead of "Characters" we find "Passions." These two books offer again an illustration of certain developing themes in the history of ideas which were to a great extent to determine the nature of later nineteenth-century literature.

First, a clarification of the terms. Passion is represented mainly by love, but it is significant that religion is also considered as one of the passions—an attitude not surprising in view of the emotion-laden overtones which Chateaubriand finds everywhere:

Christianity considered as a passion in itself, supplies the poet with immense treasures. This religious passion is all the more forceful because it contradicts all the others, and in order to endure, it must devour them. Like all great emotions it has something serious and sad about it; it makes us wander through the shadows of the cloisters and on the summits of the mountains. The beauty that a Christian adores is not a perishable beauty: it is that eternal beauty for which the disciples of Plato hastened to abandon the earth. It allows itself to be seen on earth by its adorers only in a veiled condition; it wraps itself in the folds of the universe as in a coat; for if a single one of its glances should fall directly on the heart of man, this heart could not bear it: it would burst with rapture. (II, iii, 8)

But it is perhaps the first of these two books which is the more interesting in the history of ideas. Although passion, as seen in the case of religion, can have a very particular meaning and interpretation for Chateaubriand, the concept of passion is one which has preoccupied authors from the beginning. What is new in late eighteenth- and early nineteenth-century thought is the emphasis not on the eternal and unchanging passions of man but on the specific and temporal nature of man—on his status in society. This is what Diderot referred to as "condition" and what Chateaubriand calls "character."

The entire change in focus between the Classicists and the Romanticists appears here. The passions are universal and unchanging. The social condition, on the other hand—the character, the temporary and specific items—are those whoch interest the pre-Romantic authors of the late eighteenth century and the Romantics of the nineteenth century

A glance at some of the chapter heading which list the various characters will indicate the exact nature of the phenomena Chateaubriand is discussing: husband and wife, the father, the mother, the son, the priest, the warrior.

In each cast, with the characters as with the passions, Chateaubriand chooses a literary example of the situation he describes: at times, the illustrations are drawn from antiquity; at times, from almost contemporary literature. Here again Chateaubriand is emphasizing the close relationship between philosophy and literature as he sees them: all things are bound up together, and literature can best be analyzed in the light of the principles of interaction which can be deduced from the entire context.

The importance of this focus on *character* or *condition* is that we have here the foundation of the entire concept of the nineteenth-century novel of manners in France. Balzac and Stendhal could have developed only in this current of thought. The idea seems paradoxical, since there are such great and visible differences between Chateaubriand and the two authors mentioned. To be sure, Chateaubriand did not write novels of manners, but the current of thought he represents lays the essential foundation for those later authors.

V *Poetry and Architecture*

Two final passages from Chateaubriand are of signal importance here: Part III, book I, Chapter 8, "On Gothic Churches"; and book V, chapters 3 and 4, "On Ruins In General" and "The Picturesque Effect of Ruins," respectively. Although separated in the text, they have a certain affinity.

In the two cases, it is a question of suddenly discovering a beauty where before there was seen only ugliness. In the field of Gothic architecture especially, the art had fallen into disrepute. The term itself is indicative; Gothic architecture has, in fact, nothing to do with the Goths. "Gothic," in the eighteenth century was a pejorative term more or less the equivalent of "barbarous." Throughout the Classical period, the Gothic monuments were generally considered an eyesore devoid of interest. Where possible, the old churches were abandoned, and new ones were built. Frequently when this was not possible, the old church was remodeled to eliminate some of the distasteful elements. It remained for the late eighteenth century to discover the beauty inherent in Gothic art. From the very first, Chateaubriand was one of the propagandists for Gothic art, and he was certainly the most eloquent.

Ruins, of all types of architecture, which had formerly been seen only as debris cluttering up the landscape, suddenly took on hitherto unseen beauty. The vogue of ruins actually went so far that the owners of estates unfortunate enough not to possess any authentic ruins actually commissioned architects to construct ruins. Some of these made-to-order ruins are still to be seen today, as in the Parc Monceau in Paris.

In literature, churches and ruins start to take over an important role in the development of almost any work: the hero regularly stops to visit an old church or sits down to meditate on a broken bit of column or lintel.

For Gothic, the explanation is simple: in its rejection of medieval literature and manners, the French Classicists had found medieval art equally blameworth. Each literary period in general dislikes what immediately preceded it. Time and perspective are needed to allow an individual to assess the true worth of something. This beginning of perspective was the state at which both art and literature had arrived by the late eighteenth century. Formerly despised bits of architecture could now be appreciated. In the case of the non-Gothic ruins, new discoveries made by travelers to the Middle East suddenly turned the attention of the public to these physical remnants of the civilizations of the past.[4] The enormous archeological enthusiasm generated by Napoleon's campaign in Egypt reinforced this "rediscovery" of ruins to a great extent.

In both cases, however, it is not so much the esthetic beauty of the architecture which is important; it is the evocative possibilities of the churches and ruins which interest Chateaubriand:

All men have a secret attraction to ruins. This feeling derives from the fragility of our nature—a secret conformity between these ruined monuments and the rapidity of our existence. Allied to that is the idea which consoles us for our smallness, since we see that whole peoples, men who were on occasion so famous, were unable for all that to survive the few days assigned to our obscurity. (III, ii, 3)

Of course, this is not a phenomenon limited to Chateaubriand; it is European in its scope. The same sentiment is betrayed in Shelley's "Ozymandias":

> I met a traveller from an antique land
> Who said: Two vast and trunkless legs of stone
> Stand in the desert. Near them, on the sand,
> Half sunk, a shattered visage lies, whose frown,
> And wrinkled lip, and sneer of cold command,
> Tell that its sculptor well those passions read
> Which yet survive, stamped on these lifeless things,
> The hand that mocked them and the heart that fed:
> And on the pedestal these words appear:
> "My name is Ozymandias, King of Kings:
> Look on my works, ye Mighty, and despair!"
> Nothing beside remains. Round the decay
> Of that collossal wreck, boundless and bare
> The lone and level sands stretch far away.

The extent to which these phenomena are interpreted by "poetic" rather than by factual considerations is as clear in Chateaubriand as in Shelley. Several things in Shelley could be attacked on factual grounds: Egyptian statuary is characterized by the serenity of the portraiture—the sneer is strictly in Shelley's imagination; moreover, the inscription has been modified to suit the poet's fancy; finally, the fragment mentioned is actually located in the midst of the most impressive remnants of a temple. Portrayed realistically, the scene would have furnished the materials for a far different poem where the irony of contrast between the inscription and the barren landscapes would be nonexistent.

Just so, Chateaubriand in his chapter on Gothic architecture creates a completely fanciful history of the development of the style—a history which is entirely impressionistic. He bases his discussion on the associations which he seems to see in the many emotions which assail him as he gazes on a Gothic church. The true history of architectural development was either unknown to Chateaubriand or he chose deliberately to ignore it. The latter seems more probable. Here as elsewhere Chateaubriand is seeking a poetic truth which often has little or nothing to do with actual truth. Suffice it to say that each of the elements of Gothic architecture mentioned by Chateaubriand had its origin in a specific physical need: to hold up the walls, to supply a roof that would not catch fire, and the like.

Here is what this rather banal history of development becomes with Chateaubriand:

Everything must be in its place, a truth which is commonplace from being so often repeated, but without which, after all, there can be nothing perfect. The Greeks would no more have liked an Egyptian temple at Athens than the Egyptians would have liked a Greek temple at Memphis. These two monuments in different locations would have lost their principal beauty, that is to say their ties with the institutions and the mores of the peoples. For us this reflection is applied to the old monuments of Christianity. It is curious to note that even in this century of unbelievers the poets and novelists, by a natural return to the manners of our ancestors, are pleased to introduce into their fictions tunnels, phantoms, castles, Gothic churches: such is the charm of memories which are bound up with the religion and the history of the homeland! . . .

In vain will they build elegant Greek temples, filled with light, to gather together the *good people* of Saint Louis and make them adopt a *metaphysical* God—they will always miss these cathedrals of Notre Dame of Rheims and Paris, these mossy basilicas filled with generations of dead and the soul of their fathers; they will always miss a Montmorency tomb, on which they *were wont* to kneel during Mass, not forgetting the sacred fonts where they were carried at their birth. The fact is that all those things are essentially bound to our mores; a monument has value only to the extent that a long history of the past is, so to speak, indelibly imprinted beneath the time-blackened vaults. That is why there is nothing marvelous in a church you have seen built and whose echos and domes have been formed before our eyes. God is eternal Law; His origin and all that which has to do with His ministry must lose itself in the dark of time. . . .

The forests were the first temples of Divinity, and men took from the forests their inspiration for architecture. Thus the art necessarily varied according to the climate. The Greeks formed the elegant Corinthian column with its capital of leaves modeled on the palm tree. The enormous pillars of the old Egyptian style represent the sycamore, the oriental fig tree, the banana tree, and most of the giant trees of Africa and Asia.

The forest of the Gauls in turn passed into the churches of our fathers, and our forests of oaks have thus preserved their sacred origin. The vaults carved like leaves, the buttresses which support the walls and end abruptly like broken trunks, the coolness of the vaults, the darkness of the sanctuary, the obscure side-aisles, the secret passages, the low doors, everything in the Gothic church follows the model of the labyrinths of the woods, everything makes the beholder feel its religious horror, its mysteries and divinity. The two high towers planted at the entrance of the edifice rise up over the elms and yews of the cemetery and create a picturesque effect against the azure of the sky. At times the breaking day illuminates their twin heads; at times they seem to be caped with clouds or expanded in misty atmosphere. The birds even seem to be misled and adopt them for the trees of their forests: crows swoop around their summits and perch on their galeries. But suddenly confused sounds escape from the tops of the towers and chase away the frightened birds. The Christian architect, not content to build forests, tried, so to speak, to imitate its murmurs, and with the organ and the suspended bronze he has attached to the Gothic church the very sound of the wind and the thunder which resound through the depths of the forest. The centuries, evoked by these religious sounds, bring their ancient voices out of the breast of the stones and sigh in the vast basilica: the sanctuary growls like the lair of the ancient Sibyl, and while the bronze noisily swings over your head, the vaulted caves of death maintain their deep silence beneath your feet. (III, i, 8)

Here again Chateaubriand indicates clearly his belief in a kind of relativity, a kind of interaction among the various elements which go to make up a given environment. The monument, he says, takes on its fullest meaning only within a specific frame of reference, hence the anomaly of a Greek temple on French soil.

The role of Chateaubriand as one of the prime movers in the rehabilitation of Gothic art and architecture has already been mentioned. This enthusiasm for the medieval art causes him to be shocked when he looks at the recent architecture he has seen in Paris. The obvious examples of "Greek" art in Paris are of course the Pantheon, originally the church of St. Genevieve, built from 1758 to 1789, and the church of the Madeleine, begun in 1764 and not finished until 1842. It both these cases Chateaubriand could quite literally have seen the buildings rise. The effect, he finds, is entirely different from that felt on view-

ing a monument consecrated by time and endowed with a host
of associations.

In a very modern sense, Chateaubriand calls the imagination
into play to enhance the artistic value of a piece of architecture.
It is not alone what the beholder sees, but what he knows about
the building, that creates the total emotion felt by him.

From this evocation of the historical associations that come
from a knowledge of the events that had taken place in the old
churches, the tombs to be found there, the deeds done by those
associated with the church, Chateaubriand moves even further
afield to paint his fanciful picture of the origins of Gothic art,
which this time has nothing to do with actual associations, but
by mere suggestions of associations.

In point of fact, the development of Gothic art is entirely
clear-cut in its main lines. The Roman basilica, or market, not
a religious building at all, was the original model of the Christian church. A transept was added to increase the size and to
symbolize the cross. The flat wooden roof, which caught fire
easily, was replaced, when technically possible, by a stone vault.
Further development of the vault allowed better construction
through the adding of ribs which compartmentalized the long
vault into smaller squares and geometrical patterns. As time
went on, the ribs were to become more and more ornate in a
natural scheme of development. The walls, originally very
thick, a necessity for holding up the vault, gradually became
thinner as it was discovered that occasional buttresses, that is
thick places in the walls, could substitute for the massive wall of
the earlier churches. Finally, by design or accident, the pointed
arch was discovered. Its important advantage of allowing greater
height, brought about its rapid dominance.

Chateaubriand chooses to disregard a scientific explanation
of the origins to give full reign to his fancy. In fact, he probably
did not know in detail the true development of the art, but he
seems certainly to be aware of the impressionistic nature of what
he says, admitting in a footnote that his personal explanation
does not agree with that of certain authorities.

What does Chateaubriand choose then to see in the Gothic
cathedral? He sees the ancient forests where the druids practiced
their worship, and where more recently, the fugitive priests,
evading the revolutionaries, celebrated mass far from the

churches and the cities. The ribs and decorations of the vaults
(especially of the English churches—Chateaubriand was writing
this in England or in France soon after his return) do indeed
resemble branches and trees. It is perhaps somewhat less easy
to accept Chateaubriand literally when he compares the towers
with trees, or the sounds of the organ and bells with the forest
murmurs; but in the world of suggestion the link can be a most
tenuous one and still produce its effect.

In all this Chateaubriand is again demonstrating his conviction that imagination is superior to reality. The possessor of the
poetic soul, as he sees it, is always capable of greater insight,
greater understanding, greater appreciation, through his ability
to sense the hidden meanings, the veiled associations. As with
all poets, he considers himself a seer, one capable of penetrating
more deeply into things, and able to seize the poetic essence of
a thought or an object. This personal vision is what he attempts
to communicate to his reader.

VI *General Nature of* The Genius

Every chapter of the *Genius* would lend itself to a minute
study which would be equally revealing of the mentality of
Chateaubriand and that of his age. Studied in detail, the work
must necessarily fall into an infinite number of small pieces,
each complete in itself and different from all the others. And yet
on the level of general and universal considerations there are certain recurring themes such as the importance of religion as paramount in the soul of man. The Christian religion has untapped
potentialities in the area of literary inspiration. Here we might
enter into a digression to allude to a literary quarrel still far
from solved today: the "sincerity" of the author. Is it necessary
for the author to be convinced of the fundamental truth of his
writings in order to be a great author? Chateaubriand would no
doubt tend to answer yes, with some modifications. The classics
were great since their religion was at the basis of their work. A
modern author who considers the ancient religions as mythology
cannot have this same commitment. The modern author therefore has an interest in using as his literary foundation the mysteries of the Christian religion.

But on a still more general level, whether Chateaubriand
invokes religion, art, architecture, nature, anything—what is of

overpowering importance everywhere is the suggestive possibilities of the phenomenon. The new *sensibilité* of the early nineteenth-century author requires that by a kind of intuitive and subconscious leap he be able to progress rapidly and freely from the visible realities to the psychological domain of suggestion.

CHAPTER 4

Two Epics and a Book of Travels:
The Martyrs, The Natchez,
Itinerary from Paris to Jerusalem

I *The Modern Epic*

FOR some reason, a large proportion of the great French authors, and likewise untold numbers of the nongreat, felt an undeniable attraction to the epic form. Chateaubriand was no exception in following in this tradition. From the very beginning of modern French literature, the epic form had been a preferred one. In the sixteenth century, Ronsard composed his *Franciade,* presumably the epic retelling of the founding of France. Voltaire in the enlightenth century produced his *Henriade* whose epic hero was Henri IV. A sure sign of the widespread exploitation of the form, satires of the genre were numerous in all of Europe, as evidenced by Pope's *Dunciad,* Tassoni's *Rape of the Bucket,* and the French satires such as the *Travesty of Vergil* by the seventeenth-century author Scarron, who parodied in it the early portion of the *Aeneid.*

This extraordinary authority of the epic in France, as in all of Europe, is easy to explain. First, education was then, and continued until relatively recently, to be very much oriented toward the classics. Even in the early years of the twentieth century, Lycée students all studied Latin and Greek, and advanced students at the Sorbonne were encouraged to write one of their two theses in Latin. In looking at almost any of the works of Chateaubriand, we can immediately sense the ever-present force of the classic texts. Not only had Chateaubriand thoroughly read the ancients and translated a goodly number of them, but his memory was good enough that he was never at a loss to quote an appropriate phase from Horace or Vergil.[1]

Almost any cultured Frenchman then had the examples of the

Iliad, the *Odyssey,* and the *Aeneid* constantly before his eyes as models. If other models were needed, the Italians, whose literature had long and deep influence in France, continued to produce epics in quantity, both serious and comic: Ariosto's *Orlando furioso,* Tasso's *Jerusalem Delivered,* and Pulci's *Morgante.* There were English models, too. Chateaubriand's admiration for Milton's *Paradise Lost* is proved by the careful translation of the text he was to make late in his career. Further evidence of this admiration is found in the frequent allusion to Milton by Chateaubriand, particularly in the opening of *The Martyrs.* It is only natural, therefore, that the epic, which had proved a most successful form of the long narrative, should continue to be deemed a proper vehicle of expression.

A second consideration is also important. Before the nineteenth century the novel had not been a dominant and serious genre. True, there are some outstanding examples of French seventeenth- and especially eighteenth-century novels, but they represent the exception far more than the rule. The typical novel of the early years of modern French literature was a long, formless ramble that was scorned by most of the serious writers.[2] Therefore, if an author wished to present a long narrative, the epic was the only model available.

These modern imitations of the classical epics were for the most part failures in the eyes of posterity. Voltaire's *Henriade* was extremely popular at the time, but it is only a historical curiosity for us. Likewise, no one reads the *Franciade* today.

Here is a place where Chateaubriand offers a sharp contrast with his predecessors. Not only are his two epics still highly readable, but they may easily count among his best works. Unfortunately, the general avoidance of "modern" epics on the part of readers has harmed the works—too often they are condemned without having been read. Thus, it will be all the more important to examine these two works in some detail, together with the book of travels which was the "by-product" of the preparation of one of the epics.

II *Chateaubriand's Epics*

The two epics are *The Martyrs* and *The Natchez;* the *Itinerary from Paris to Jerusalem* in a sense bears the same relation to *The Martyrs* that the *Travels in America* bears to *The Natchez;*

that is, it is the more or less fanciful relation of an extensive trip which was to serve as background for another work. Chateaubriand's success in this area is the direct result of his personality, his education, and his writer's technique. If there was ever an author whose talents suited him for writing epics, it was Chateaubriand. The majesty of his prose and the enormous scope of his view of the universe are precisely the materials needed to compose a perfect epic.

Surprisingly, we can deal with the two epics together, in spite of their vast difference in subject. This is because in both cases Chateaubriand was drawing on an identical epic force which retained its identity in spite of its application in two different eras, on two different civilizations, on two different continents. The particular elements of *The Natchez* which have to do specifically with the American setting will be considered separately in Chapter 5, on "Chateaubriand's America." Suffice to say here that Chateaubriand's America is a vast act of literary creation which bears no resemblance to a faithful and accurate depiction. The very magnitude of this creation justifies the epic treatment.

Although chronologically the publication of *The Natchez* comes several years after *The Martyrs,* the dates of their composition were not so distinctly separated. *The Natchez* indeed can be traced back to the days of the trip to America (1791) and the time of service in the Army of the Princes followed by the exile in England, since the massive manuscript Chateaubriand had been elaborating since those days was the fountainhead of the epic. Both were likewise to a great extent the fruit of *The Genius of Christianity.* It will be remembered that one of the dominant themes in that work was the renovation of the classical forms through a use of nonclassical themes. In the two epics the renovating themes were to be the use of two particular subject matters—Christian religious history and the exoticism of settings and characters. In writing these monumental works, Chateaubriand is in a sense attempting to prove by his example the ideas he had put forward in the *Genius.* As can be seen, the "renovation" was based on a firm foundation according to Chateaubriand's theory—he considered the history of the early Christian martyrs as an infinitely more emotional subject for a work of art than the classic tales and myths, especially for an early nineteenth-century French reader who was involved in the turmoil of intense religious revival. In the same way a strongly exotic subject matter was ideally suited to an age so anxious to see all that was most strange and unusual pictorially represented.

The first of the works to appear was *The Martyrs*, published in 1809. To do the groundwork for his epic, Chateaubriand felt it was necessary to visit the areas in which the events forming his chosen subject actually took place, and in 1806 he set out on a trip which was to take him to Greece, Turkey, Palestine, Egypt, Tunisia, and finally a return to France through Spain. It will be remembered that the end of this pilgrimage, the travels in Spain, was to be the inspiration for *The Last Abencerraje*.

In making this trip, Chateaubriand was not being quite as unconventional as he had been a few years earlier in setting out for America "to discover the Northwest passage." However, it was still a remarkable voyage for 1806. Not many writers had yet undertaken the trials and tribulations of such a trip. Undeniably, at the time Chateaubriand took the trip it was still a frightening undertaking, fraught with peril. The plague was always rampant in the Middle East at those times, and robbers and religious fanatics were ever ready to attack the infidel traveler. Chateaubriand's safe-conduct firman from the sultan is still preserved in the French National Library, but it is noteworthy that the sultan had no delusions about the force of his name—the document authorized Chateaubriand to raise a band of armed guards to protect him. Another factor that cannot be overlooked is the extreme cost of such an undertaking, especially for a member of a relatively impoverished family of the old nobility. Recent research on Chateaubriand's financial situation seems to indicate that the trip to the Middle East cost him, in terms of today's purchasing power, perhaps fifty to one hundred thousand dollars. It is no wonder, then, that it was looked upon as a great adventure. In the years following Chateaubriand, however, and to a great extent as a result of his writings, travels in the Orient were to become almost as commonplace, almost as necessary to any well-bred young man's education, as had been the eighteenth-century Englishman's Grand Tour of France and Italy.

It would be misleading to look only for firsthand visual sources in the development of *The Martyrs*. Characteristically, Chateau-

briand read all that was available on the subect and digested it
thoroughly, forming an enormous dossier of materials upon
which to draw. Since a part of the narrative was to be laid in
medieval Gaul, he undertook extensive studies of the historians
and observers such as Sidonius Apollinaris.

After the composition of the epic, there remained vast sheaves
of notes covering both the trip and the readings. The leftovers
served to form the book of travels, *Itinerary from Paris to Jerusalem,* finally published in 1811.

The Natchez, based on an early eighteenth-century uprising of
the Natchez and the subsequent massacre of the French, was a
constant preoccupation of his from the early days. Both *Atala*
and *René* were originally drawn from the still formless manuscript of *The Natchez,* and certain passages, especially descriptions of the American countryside, had passed into other works:
The Essay on Revolutions, The Genius of Christianity. The work
did not appear in finished form, however, until 1826, as part of
the *Complete Works* which began publication that year. Even
as published, certain aspects of it suggest there had not been time
to complete the work as originally planned. The first half is in
epic style, divided into books, while the second half is in more
natural narrative style and divided into chapters.

This strange form may, however, be the result of a realization
by Chateaubriand that there was no longer the great distinction
between epic and novel that there had been in the past and that,
indeed, the novel was to be the form of the future.

The Natchez, expanded beyond the historic incident of the
massacre of the French, is transformed in Chateaubriand's hands
into a vast uprising of the Indians against the white man. The
temptation is to make an immediate comparison with the reactions of the ancient Gauls under the Roman occupation as
described in *The Martyrs,* and indeed it is easy to see here the
type of vast confrontation which stirs Chateaubriand's imagination and inspires him. Just as he is so frequently given to establishing his descriptive comparisons on a vast level of Old World
versus the New World, of classic times versus modern times, he
is seldom content to deal with an individual in these epic works,
but feels called upon to wield whole races, whole civilizations
in his massive juxtapositions.

Before attempting to deal with the two epics in a general way, let us look into the nature of the three individual works.

III The Martyrs

The Martyrs takes place at the time of Diocletian, Roman emperor from 284 to 305. The last years of his reign were marked by persecution of the Christians, and these years came to be known as the "Age of Martyrs." It is against this background that the action of *The Martyrs* takes place.

Eudore is a young soldier who has embraced Christianity. He meets the young Greek pagan girl, Cymodocée. At this point, in typical epic style, there is a flashback in which the soldier tells her of his earlier adventures in Rome, England, and Gaul. One of the episodes of the stay in Gaul involves the most attractive portrait of the druidess Velléda who commits suicide for love of Eudore.

The young soldier falls in love with Cymodocée, but he will not make her his wife until she becomes a Christian. They separate, Eudore going to Rome and Cymodocée to Jerusalem. It is at this point that the persecutions of Diocletian begin, and the epic ends with the matyrdom of the two young people joined together in death.

The work begins with the traditional invocation to the Muse:

I wish to sing the battles of the Christians and the victory which the faithful enjoyed over the spirits of the abyss, through the glorious efforts of a martyred couple.

Celestial Muse, you who inspired the poet of Sorrento [Tasso] and the blind man of Albion [Milton], you who place your solitary throne on the Thabor [site of the transfiguration of Christ], you who delight in severe thoughts and sublime and grave meditations, I now implore your help. (Book I)

The typical epic beginning of the action has already been mentioned, the device whereby the story begins *in medias res,* with a subsequent recounting by the hero of his previous adventures. The language is not the poetry of the classical and Italian epics, but rather prose. Yet it is a lofty and noble prose which is quite in keeping with the epic genre. A modern critic thus characterizes the language: "It was no longer the prose of the eighteenth century, nor the language of Voltaire; rather it possessed, to a degree unattained even by the best pages of *Atala* and the *Genius,* force of imagery, intensity of emotion, harmonious cadences, mastery of technique and equilibrium completely without equal."[3]

Aside from the technical, and perhaps to a certain extent external, attributes of the epic style of narration—division into books, apostrophe of the muses—there are two other essentials. First, a national hero as subject. Eudore fills this requirement admirably. As one of the first martyrs, he belongs to that exalted realm of history that has been transmuted into something of a higher order. But the subject must be not only terrestrial and human. The epic demands the element of the supernatural, the marvelous. However, instead of the gods of Greece and Rome, Chateaubriand draws upon Christian metaphysics. The description of heaven, for example, indicates the nature of these developments in Chateaubriand:

Delightful gardens extend about Jerusalem the radiant. A river flows from the throne of the Almighty; it waters the Celestial Paradise, and carries on its waves pure love and the wisdom of God. . . .

The light which brightens these fortunate retreats is made of the rosy colors of morning, the flame of midday and the deep red of evening; yet no luminary appears on the resplendent horizon; no sun rises, no sun sets in these places where nothing finishes and nothing begins. . . .

Forever gathered together there, are the mortals who have practised virtue on earth; the patriarchs, seated beneath golden palm trees; the prophets with their foreheads shining with two rays of light . . . the martyrs, dressed in brilliant robes; the virgins crowned with the roses of Eden. . . . (Book III)

The story of Velléda, already referred to, forms a separate entity. In this it resembles the many episodes of the classical epic, but it resembles also the general style of Chateaubriand's writing in inserting short episodes in a larger narrative. Not only in *Atala* and *René* do we find examples, but even in the *Memoirs* it is a constant technique. Thus Velléda forms an episode which does not necessarily have to be treated in relation with the rest of the work. This story is particularly noteworthy since the character of Velléda seems in many ways to incarnate the "Sylphide" of Chateaubriand's boyhood imagination:

She wore a golden sickle hung on a bronze chain, and she was crowned with an oak branch. The whiteness of her arms and her complexion, her blue eyes, her red lips, her long blond hair, hanging loose, branded her as a daughter of the Gauls, and contrasted in their softness with her proud and savage demeanor. In a melodious voice she sang frightful words, and her uncovered breast rose and fell like the foam on the waves. (Book IX)

The comparison of this ideal of beauty with Atala is obvious.

The episode as a whole, as indeed the entire epic, has intimate bonds with religion. Again, as in *Atala* and *René*, as well as *The Abencerraje*, two lovers are separated by religion: Eudore is a Christian, Velléda is a druidess faithful to the ancient rites of the forest. In the main narrative, Cymodocée is likewise a pagan at the beginning, and even after her conversion, it is their religion and the resultant persecution of Diocletian which precipitates the final tragedy.

Chateaubriand has been faithful to his precept of utilizing religion as a source of literary inspiration. As he had predicted in *The Genius of Christianity*, Christian religious history has over paganism the advantage of drawing on the deep conviction and faith of the reader, instead of presenting him with a classical fable patently belonging to the realm of myth.

IV *The Book of Travels*

We have already mentioned the unusual nature of Chateaubriand's travels in the Orient at that time. Later, all the writers followed suit: Lamartine, Nerval, Fromentin. But again in 1806 the enterprise was new and hazardous. Obviously, the public would be interested in a straightforward book of travels. It was thus that the trip to Jerusalem produced two works of such different nature.

He says in the introduction to the *Itinerary from Paris to Jerusalem*:

I did not undertake my trip in order to write about it; I had another purpose, and I fulfilled that purpose in *The Martyrs*. I went in search of images—that is all.

I beg the reader to look upon this *Itinerary* less as a trip than as *Memoirs* of a year of my life. . . . I have no pretensions to knowing intimately the peoples of the countries I did nothing but pass through.

A moment suffices for the landscape painter to sketch a tree, outline a perspective, draw a ruin. . . .[4]

The work has the characteristics of Chateaubriand's other travel books: it is anecdotal, vague, often inaccurate. But Chateaubriand does possess that gift of the painter which allows him in a sketch to resume all the characteristic and necessary elements of the scene he is painting. His view is not an accurate, photographic view, but it is a vision which has profound insight. This is the value, the utility, the interest of the work from the esthetic point of view.

From the historical point of view, it marked in large part the opening of the Middle East to the consciousness of the Western European. The eighteenth and early nineteenth centuries were an era of discovery for the ordinary Frenchman. All of the outside world which had been largely ignored, was now thrusting itself upon the consciousness of the Frenchman: America, the Indies, East and West, the Near East and the Far East.

Chateaubriand, then, stands for his entire generation when he wanders meditating through the ruins of Greece, Egypt, and Carthage, when he speculates on the site of ancient Sparta, when he deduces the psychology of an ancient people from his sight of the Pyramids.

The second epic, *The Natchez,* deals rather with the exotic vision of America which Chateaubriand had elaborated.

V The Natchez

The action of *The Natchez* begins immediately after the events described by René. Attempting to find consolation in travel and nature, René has fled to America. The work opens with a typical epic apostrophe:

In the shade of the American forests, I wish to sing the airs of solitude as mortal ears have never heard them; I wish to relate your misfortunes, O Natchez, O Louisiana, of which only memories remain. (Book I)

René canoes up the Mississippi, stopping at an Indian village. There he meets Chactas, hero of *Atala,* who will later recount his adventures subsequent to the death of Atala and the end of the novella. A young Indian girl, Céluta, falls in love with René, but his melancholy will not allow him to participate in the joys of the world. Ondouré, himself a suitor for Céluta's hand swears vengeance on René, but in hand-to-hand battle René is victor. However, he spares Ondouré's life.

Following his classical models, Chateaubriand wishes to introduce here another requisite of the classical epics, the marvelous. Book IV transports the reader into the realm of the supernatural, where we see Saint Catherine intercede with the Virgin Mary on behalf of the Christian Indians.

We soon return to America, however, and Chactas takes this opportunity to tell of his adventures. Among the most curious of these is his trip to France, where he had been sent as a kind of Indian ambassador. He soon finds himself in jail, however, accused of treason. This Paris interlude allows Chateaubriand to enter into a field which had long fascinated writers: the perspective afforded by the view of French society taken through the ideas of a foreigner or a savage. Just as Montesquieu had criticized French society through the words of his pseudo-Persian visitors to France, in the *Persian Letters,* just as Voltaire had used the pretext of an Iroquois visitor in *The Ingenuous One* to satirize society, Chateaubriand used this means of social comment. Chactas' prison companion says to him:

Chactas, you are a savage, and I am a civilized man. Apparently you are an honest man, and I am a scoundrel. Is it not singular that you come straight from America to be my companion in chains in Europe, to show liberty and slavery, vice and virtue attached to the same yoke? That, my dear Iroquois, is Society. Isn't that a fine thing?[5]

Chactas reacts violently to this discourse: "What is, I said to myself, this strange nation, where the insane seem to have studied in the school of wisdom, and where scoundrels bear pain as they would enjoy pleasure?" (Book V).

Chactas is delivered from prison by action of the king himself, almost a reminiscence of the deus ex machina of Molière's *Tartuffe* where all is set right by the king's fiat. Chactas is taken to court, where he faces Louis XIV in person.

This gives rise to one of the "coincidences" of which Chateaubriand is so fond. Chateaubriand had carefully noted in the earlier part of the text that the chief of the Natchez was referred to as the Sun. Naturally, since he is the great Chief of the French, the king is addressed by Chactas as "Sun." Chateaubriand leaves to the reader the delightful coincidence of the savage title

of Sun being applied to Louis XIV, the Sun King. This phenomenon is exactly the same as the stylistic question of periphrasis.
French eighteenth-century rhetoric had made enormous use of
this device, whereby instead of using the specific word applicable
to a person or a thing, a roundabout means of expressing the
same thing was employed. Rather than speak of the moon, an
author might choose to speak of the "vaporous chariot of the
Queen of night." The stylistic value of the device was in allowing
the author to avoid the old, overused words and expressions and
to substitute new ones for them. The delight of the author given
to this mode of expression can well be imagined when he discovers the same process being used in the Indian languages: a
girl of eighteen summers, the month of the harvest, and the like.
The same tendency is pointed out by Chateaubriand in relation
to certain universal verities which seem to exist everywhere. True
religion, in the eye of Chateaubriand, makes itself felt even in
the mythology of the Indians. These "coincidences" of primitive man and civilized man take on great meaning for Chateaubriand—to him they prove the hand of providence.

Chactas's confrontation with the Sun of the French allows
further opportunity for social comment, and even lighthearted
fun (Chactas pushes his peace pipe under the nose of Louis XIV,
who turns pale at the smell and has to be led away).

One of the curious aspects of this Paris trip is the occasion
Chateaubriand takes to present a real historical novel, with the
great figures of literature and history taking a role: the king,
Bossuet, Turenne, Condé. Since this is in what would appear
to be the earlier portion of the manuscript, it thus seems logical
to place Chateaubriand in the vanguard of the new developments in the field of the historical novel. A few years later, Balzac
was to use this same technique of actual persons intermingled
with the fictional ones, on a massive scale.

After further sightseeing in the French capital and visits with
some of the literary greats, Chactas returns to America. Meanwhile, Ondouré, whose life René had spared, has fomented war
between the Illinois and the Natchez. In battle, René is made
prisoner but is delivered at the last minute.

Here begins the second part of the work, no longer written
in the "epic" style but in a form closer to the novel. René marries
Céluta almost as a matter of form, although he still does not

love her. A daughter is born to them whom René calls Amélie after his sister. However, Ondouré has continued his machinations, and René is arrested by the European authorities for conspiracy. He is finally released, only to learn of the death of his sister. Chactas asks him for the story of his troubles, and presumably here is where the story of *René* would be inserted into the larger work.

Ondouré's vengeance continues: on the eve of the Indian uprising, assassins kill René in the arms of Céluta. The Indians are defeated and driven from their lands.

VI *Lasting Influences of the Epic*

Certainly the epic is outmoded in today's world, but only in a sense. For indeed the epic inspiration has to a great extent penetrated the novel. To be sure, portions of Chateaubriand's epics are unreadable for the modern audience, particularly those most obvious physical and structural elements which, for the novice, serve as the outward means of identifying an epic: invocation of the Muse, division into books, use of the marvelous. This does not mean, however, that the works as a whole are today unworthy of our consideration. On the contrary, *The Natchez* and *The Martyrs* are almost certainly among Chateaubriand's masterpieces, in spite of the relative oblivion into which they seem to have fallen.

Indeed, for the reader who takes the time to examine them carefully, they will prove to be first-rate examples of Chateaubriand's art, and monuments in the history of the development of the novel. Again, it must be emphasized that the novel was still, in the time of Chateaubriand, in its infancy. To all intents and purposes, it was still a minor genre which did not deserve the attention of an important writer. It is true we can find many exceptions to this in the eighteenth century, and even in the seventeenth, but it has been only in recent times that perspective has allowed even the beginnings of an assessment of the importance of the novel before the nineteenth century. Certainly to the contemporary, the few masterpieces that now are clearly visible were hidden from the view of most. Just as the theater was undergoing a complete upheaval and reorganization in the course of the eighteenth century, the novel was doing likewise, but at a slower pace, and against heavier odds. The theater had long been a major and respected genre; the novel had not.

Thus, Chateaubriand saw the epic form as the only possible framework for a vast prose work of literature, and he believed that his technique must therefore conform to the classical dictates of physical presentation. It is clear, however, that Chateaubriand was modifying the form as he went along. The most startling aspect of this change is to be found of course in *The Natchez*, which, halfway through, abandons the pseudo-epic form to become a straightforward narration. Chateaubriand's modifications of the epic seem here almost to mirror what Voltaire did nearly a century earlier in regard to the theater: he took the form of the classical tragedy, and while respecting the basic framework of the rules and traditions, so modified them in the detail that a new esthetic evolved.

The Martyrs is perhaps more difficult of acceptance for the modern reader educated outside the influence of French tradition. The classical associations, the religious associations, do not have the same impact which they had on the readers of Chateaubriand's day. In spite of this, it is still a book to be admired. But that very statement can be damning, for something that is admired is thereby removed from the immediacy of response which is necessary if the proper effect is to be achieved.

The Natchez, on the other hand, may well deserve to be near the top of any list of masterpieces. In spite of some of the faded attributes of the epic, it remains as a novel a work capable of fascinating the reader. Again, it is necessary to avoid any attempt at seeking a "realistic" portrayal of the American scene and its inhabitants. Rather, the work is a vast canvas filled with forceful descriptions, painted with a myriad of brilliant colors, transmitting at the same time a psychologically faithful portrait of all the attributes of the Romantic soul. All this is couched in what is truly a masterpiece of stylistic expression.

Chateaubriand's epics may be considered as the fountainhead of that long series of modern long novels, epic in their scope, which are not content to paint the inner feelings of a very restricted number of protagonists, but which rather find it necessary to deal with vast forces, overwhelming movements, and vast waves of sentiment and passion.

CHAPTER 5

Chateaubriand's America

I Special Nature of the Portrayal

MUCH has been left unsaid in the preceding chapters; time and again, much more needed to be said concerning Chateaubriand's very particular portrayal of America, which by the enormous influence of the works, became the vision of generations of Europeans in connection with the New World. Whether the work under discussion is *Atala, The Natchez, René,* the *Travels in America,* or the countless other works where America seems to be a constantly returning theme, the same remarks are applicable. At this point, then, rather than dealing with each work individually, we shall take up the entire question of Chateaubriand's America, in an attempt to assess precisely what is the nature of his evocation and why it is so.

Until very recent times, most critics have been guilty of failure to make the effort necessary to understand Chateaubriand's America, for understanding and appreciating these concepts is not an easy task. Especially as regards his paintings of America, he certainly does not today occupy that universally admired position to which he is entitled. A number of reasons can be cited, no doubt, for this state of affairs, but they can be reduced to one simple statement: lack of comprehension. The necessity, on the part of many Americans, to approach Chateaubriand through translation is the cause for one kind of incomprehension: certainly, without the stylistic element of Chateaubriand's flowing and mellifluous phrases, no true evaluation can be made. But even for the French-reading public of the universities there is a sad lack of understanding of what Chateaubriand can mean to the modern world. Out of precaution, it must be stated at this juncture that Chateaubriand in the modern world is not at all Chateaubriand as he appeared to his contemporaries. Indeed, Chateaubriand himself might be quite surprised

89

to hear attributed to him some of the qualities which a twentieth-century critic can attempt to find in him. But there is no doubt that he has a meaning and a value which infinitely transcend the simplistic understanding afforded the works by their contemporaries.

As a final proof of the lack of comprehension of the worth and interest of the author, we can cite the fate of *Atala* as a beginning French reading text. *Atala* is a difficult enough work for an advanced student who has a certain amount of literary sophistication; its effect on the beginner can be disastrous. There is a distinction to be made between a bare-comprehension level, on which terms *Atala* can be considered a simple text, and a level of true appreciation, which is a difficult task indeed.

Masquerading as a simple text, then, *Atala* is bound to be misunderstood. But there is a further misunderstanding. Since *Atala* is a tale of American Indian life, it is exceedingly appropriate, in theory at least, that this should be presented as a text for American students. But especially at the beginning stages, the reader tends to be excessively literal-minded. Under such scrutiny, the book can only be considered an accumulation of worthless nonsense. All this comes from a failure to understand what Chateaubriand's America was. This is what we should attempt to discover.

The failures of comprehension in Chateaubriand criticism can perhaps be reduced to two general causes: the extreme literalness we have just seen, and envy. We shall have frequent occasion to return to the question of literalness. As for envy, the word is perhaps ill-chosen, but no other seems to suffice. An illustration can be drawn from a typical review of one of the significant new works of Chateaubriand's criticism: "This grandiloquent little man appears through his voluminous writings as a kind of officious Ossian, the mini-Homer of the dawning age of Cooks tours."[1] The difficulty is that Chateaubriand's personality does evoke precisely this kind of response. Everyone is eager to catch the master in a mistake, to prove him a liar or a plagiarist. Every opportunity is seized to make him look ridiculous.

Far from avoiding this practice, let us indulge in it, at least for the moment, on the excuse of giving a concrete example. On his trip to America, Chateaubriand was traveling on a tiny cod-fishing brigantine that lends itself very poorly to the magnificent evocations of such scenes as the seascape of the "Two Perspectives of Nature" in *The Genius of Christianity*.[2] But the true state of affairs could not be deduced from Chateaubriand's descriptions: it is only through the patient research of the scholars that the poetic bark is reduced to the smelly fishing boat. One of the "harrowing" experiences of the crossing is Chateaubriand's near-drowning. Here is how he describes the adventure:

When I landed at Saint-Pierre, the capital of the island consisted, as best I remember, of a fairly long street built along the sea. The gracious inhabitants were quick to offer us the hospitality of their tables and homes. The governor lived at the edge of the city. I dined two or three times there. He was raising a few European vegetables in one of the moats of the fort. I remember that after dinner he would show me his garden; then we would go sit at the base of the flagpole surmounting the fortress. The French flag billowed over our heads, as we watched a wild sea and the somber coasts of Newfoundland, and spoke of the homeland.

After a two-week layover, we left the island of Saint-Pierre, and the ship heading south reached the latitude of the coasts of Maryland and Virginia, where we were becalmed. We enjoyed the most beautiful of skies; the nights, the sunsets, and sunrises were admirable. In the chapter of *The Genius of Christianity* which I have already mentioned, called "Two Perspectives of Nature," I have recalled one of those nocturnal splendors and one of those magnificent sunsets. "The sun's globe, ready to plunge into the waves, appeared between the ship's lines, in the midst of endless space, and so on."

An accident came close to ending all my plans.

The heat was oppressive; the ship, in a dead calm, without sail, and overburdened by its masts, was rolling heavily. Burning on the deck and fatigued by the movement, I decided I wanted to swim, and although we had no longboat in the water, I threw myself from the bowsprit into the sea. First all went well, and several passengers imitated me. I was swimming without watching the ship; but when I happened to turn my head, I saw that the current had already borne it quite far away. The crew had rushed on deck and had thrown a hawser to the other swimmers. Sharks were sighted in the waters near the ship, and the crew were firing on them to drive them away. The roll was so great that it delayed my return and sapped my strength. I had an abyss beneath me, and at any moment the sharks might snap off one of my arms or legs. On the vessel, they were attempting to launch a boat, but they had to set up a block and tackle, and that was taking considerable time.

By the greatest stroke of luck, a barely perceptible breeze came up;

the ship obeyed the rudder to a certain extent and approached me. I was able to grab hold of the rope, but the companions of my rashness had also caught hold of this rope; and when we were drawn to the side of the vessel, I found myself at the end of the line, and they hung on me with all their combined weight. We were fished out this way one by one, which took a long time. The rolling continued; at each roll we would dive ten or twelve feet into the waves, or we would be suspended in the air, like fish on a line. At the last immersion, I felt ready to lose consciousness; one more roll, and it would have been all over. Finally they raised me on board half dead. If I had drowned, good riddance for myself and for others![3]

Unfortunately for the memory of Chateaubriand, however, there was on board a certain cleric, the abbé de Mondésir, who later wrote down his impressions of the crossing, with many an unpleasant word for Chateaubriand. The good abbé had been annoyed by Chateaubriand's custom of standing on the deck and declaiming passages from the Bible complete with histrionics. The hairbreadth escape was witnessed by the abbé, but as he describes it, the incident is somewhat different:

The Chevalier [Chateaubriand was still at that time known as the chevalier de Combourg], I might also say Don Quixote, who liked to take chances which were often rash, decided to take a swim in the Ocean. The sailors asked him if he had ever swum in the Ocean, and when he answered no, they vainly attempted to deter him from a dangerous fancy: they had to give in to him. They made us all, priests and levites, descend to the cabin. The bather undressed completely, they put straps under his arms, and he was thus lowered to the water. Scarcely had his feet touched, than the hero fainted, and they had to hurry to hoist him back on board, with the added fear that a shark might cut him in two. When he regained his senses on the deck, he said: "Well, now I know what it's all about."[4]

Such blatant distortion of the truth (whether by Chateaubriand or by Mondésir) can only lead to scorn for the author. Many critics have seized on just such discrepancies to denigrate Chateaubriand. The situation is further complicated by the fact that next to the violent "enemies" of Chateaubriand we invariably find the "defenders" who are no less violent. For these, the suggestion that anything but absolute truth ever came from the pen of Chateaubriand is the sin without remission.

It is these contrary emotions, interspersed from time to time with the discoveries of an occasional disinterested scientific in-

vestigator, which have made the controversy over Chateaubriand
and America so long and so bitter. At this point, the literal-
mindedness of certain critics tends to become inextricably involved with the passions: because critic X never saw any green
flamingos on the Mississippi, because critic Y has observed that
in the late summer there isn't enough water in the Ohio River
to float boats, Chateaubriand must necessarily be branded a liar.
Several facts stand out from the long polemic, and we may start
by outlining these important elements.

II *The Elaboration of the Legend*

First, Chateaubriand was the typical boastful traveler, unwilling to admit that he had not been everywhere. From the
very first, Chateaubriand boasted in his writings of having seen
everything from the far north to the southern tip of Florida. We
may well be tempted to trace this habit back to Chateaubriand's
days as a soldier in the Army of the Princes. In one passage from
the *Memoirs,* which is particularly revealing from the psychological point of view, the author says: "As we were eating out of
our mess kits under the tents, my comrades would ask me for
stories of my trips. They paid me back in tall tales; we all lied
like the corporal in the bar when the recruit is paying the
bill" (IX, 11).

All the early mentions of America, however, are merely fragments inserted into larger works: sunsets, detached nature scenes,
isolated incidents. Chateaubriand's London publisher, Colburn,
did in 1808 gather together all these passages from the works
published to that date. This he presented as a volume of travels,
but the coherent, if that is the word, relation of Chateaubriand's
travels had to await the 1826 Pourrat edtion of the *Oeuvres
complètes.*

Two considerations seem to have dictated this period for the
genesis of the *Travels in America*: in the composition of his
Memoirs, Chateaubriand had at this time (1826) reached the
point in his chronological development where he needed to
describe the travels. But, as usual, he wanted to multiply the
uses of his material. So he composed one version for the *Memoirs*
intended for posthumous publication, and one for a book to be
published immediately. The second consideration was a practical
one: in the prospectus of the Ladvocat edition he had promised

voluminous unpublished material, and so far the only sizable unpublished work to appear in the *Complete Works* was *The Natchez*.

The *Travels in America* was therefore prepared (rather hastily from all appearences). The problem Chateaubriand had to solve was how to draw up an itinerary which would tie together the earlier boasts of all the regions visited. The problem of tracing the itinerary is heightened for the scholar because of Chateaubriand's extreme vagueness in all cases where preciseness would be required.

As clearly as can be determined, Chateaubriand says in the *Travels* and in the *Memoirs* that he landed in Baltimore, visited Philadelphia, New York, Boston, and the battlefields of Lexington, and returned to New York; he then sailed up the Hudson River to Albany and went inland along the old Mohawk Trail to Niagara Falls. Then he canoed up a river, portaged to the Ohio River system, sailed down the Ohio from Pittsburgh to the Mississippi, then south along that river to the Natchez country, east to Florida, and back north through the mountains. There in a cabin he picked up a newspaper announcing the flight of Louis XVI from his semicaptivity in Paris and his arrest at Varennes. Chateaubriand immediately boarded a ship and returned to France.

There is good evidence corroborating this itinerary as far as Niagara, with the possible exception of the New York-Boston excursion, which is doubtful. From Niagara on, however, the trip becomes so extensive that, even with double the time he had at his disposal, an experienced traveler could not have made it. Time must be taken out of the itinerary for his recuperation after his arm was broken at Niagara. Furthermore. Chateaubriand says that the ship left for France at a date when no ship left. The only available ship left almost a month earlier, thus reducing even further an already short stay.

Here is the evidence supporting this part of the itinerary. The facts are few but convincing. The abbé de Mondésir's testimony corroborates te fact that Chateaubriand was actually on board the *Saint-Pierre,* the codfishing vessel which the Abbé Nagot had specially chartered to take his theology students to Baltimore where a seminary was to be established. The actual stagecoach schedule of the period fits with Chateaubriand's descriptions of the duration and nature of the trip to Philadelphia.

Chateaubriand had a letter of introduction for George Washington from the marquis de la Rouerie, who had fought with Washington during the revolution; this letter is still preserved among Washington's papers. Chateaubriand must, therefore, have presented the letter, and Chateaubriand's descriptions of Washington's Philadelphia house are authentic according to contemporary engravings and accounts.

Unfortunately for Chateaubriand's reputation once again, however, there was discovered in recent years Washington's reply to the marquis de la Rouerie. In it, he states that he regrets he was sick the day of Chateaubriand's visit and could not see him. Chateaubriand left the next day, according to Washington, who as we all know never told a lie, so that Chateaubriand's extended descriptions of his two interviews with the president are entirely fictional.

No doubt needs to be cast on the visit to New York, as it forms an essential link in the itinerary, although there is no specific evidence to support this. The pilgrimage to Boston to see the battlefields of Lexington seems rather doubtful; Chateaubriand speaks of it as one completely unaware of the great distances involved: he seems to have been plotting the itinerary on a small-scale map.

The visit to Niagara seems highly likely. In Washington's letter, the president remarks that Chateaubriand had left the next morning "for Niagara." This documents at least the intent. But there is one capital piece of information: at the time of Chateaubriand's visit, a permit from the British commander was necessary to visit the Niagara region. It was recently discovered that this commander was a Colonel Gordon. Chateaubriand makes a mistake on the grade (calling him captain), but he specifies the name of the commander. This seems almost irrefutable evidence that Chateaubriand was indeed on the spot. Gordon is not mentioned in any of the books that Chateaubriand might have consulted.

After Niagara, however, all is shrouded in mystery. If, as seems highly probable, Chateaubriand returned to France on the *Molly* out of Philadelphia, the total time for his itinerary was four and a half months. The entire itinerary after Niagara would be physically impossible. Moreover, the first point of importance on this itinerary, Pittsburgh, was under siege by the Indians, about which fact Chateaubriand says nothing. Logic seems to dictate that, starting from Pittsburgh, the itinerary was fabricated. The most probable assumption is that Chateaubriand stayed several weeks in the Niagara area, which would allow him just enough time to return to the east coast and seek out a ship to take him home after the news of the king's arrest at Varennes. Chateaubriand's tale of picking up the newspaper and reading the headline seems perhaps a bit too dramatic to be true, but a look at the newspapers of 1811 shows that the headline Chateaubriand quotes, "Flight of the King," is indeed the headline that appeared.

III *Critical Evaluation of the Trip*

For 150 years the critics have argued the pros and cons of this trip. A few were logical and accepted part of the itinerary and doubted the rest. All too many, however, either argued that Chateaubriand had never even set foot in America, or else argued that the itinerary was absolutely authentic, all but sacrosanct: not one word must be doubted.

In the course of this polemic, the discovery was made of the extent to which Chateaubriand in the *Voyage* had depended on written source material to the virtual exclusion of actual experience. Eighteenth- and nineteenth-century authors and travelers such as Lahontan, Charlevoix, Carver, Imlay, Bartram, Beltrami, and many others supplied Chateaubriand with the elements of fact, or often fiction which he took for fact, that were to be the building blocks of his recital.

The result of this long pursuit of the sources is that practically every page of the *Travels in America* has had its sources identified, but there still has been next to no work done on the importance of these sources from a literary point of view.

If one remains on the level of identifying sources, the attitude continues to be one in which we are trying to denigrate the author by denying his originality. In point of fact, the stylistic transformations that Chateaubriand works on these source materials are the most revealing and useful bits of evidence one would wish to have in approaching the only too vague subject of stylistics.

Why did Chateaubriand paint such a picture of America? Did he really think he was seeing the things he tells of? On one level, no. And yet, for anyone who lives by imagination as much as Chateaubriand did, fact and fiction, experience and reading become so intertwined that they cannot be separated. It seems certain that on many points, it would have been impossible for Chateaubriand to know whether he had or had not been a witness to the scene, especially since more than thirty years had elapsed since the experiences recounted.

The America which Chateaubriand describes is a conglomerate, a mixture, perhaps a distillate of all he had seen, all he had heard, and that he had read about America. It seems logical to assume that this synthesis of a new and personal America began at the very moment he set foot on the soil of the New World.

A close examination of what the author's first reactions were can be revealing here. There is much evidence to indicate that America was a vast disappointment to Chateaubriand. If we may return for a moment to the question of sources, one will recall the extent to which Chateaubriand had prepared for his trip by reading all of the important *voyageurs*. We are reminded of Proust's theme of disappointment with reality when it does not correspond with the preconceived notion conjured up by the place name. Chateaubriand most definitely knows what he was expecting to find in America, and he did not find it. That is most clear.

The good Quaker is legendary, both before and after Chateaubriand, and the example found in Vigny's play *Chatterton* is only one of many. Chateaubriand was completely imbued with the mythology, so to speak, of the peaceful, kind, and virtuous Quaker. What did he find in Philadelphia, the city of Quakers? Hardly what he expected.

I saw that this society which was so vaunted was, for the most part, only a company of avid merchants, without warmth and without sensitivity, who had created for themselves a reputation of honesty because they wear clothes different from the ones other people wear, never answer either yes or no, never have two scales of prices (because the monopoly of certain merchandise which they have forces you to buy from them and at whatever price they fix); in a word, they are calculating actors who are always playing a farce of probity, calculated at an enormous rate of interest, and with whom truth is an affair of speculation.[5]

It is noteworthy that this bitter passage comes from the *Essay on Revolutions,* which belongs to a period much closer to the American adventure than *The Natchez* or the *Travels in America* or even *Atala.* It belongs, it would appear, to the period when the disappointment was strongest and before the imaginary America of the later works had completely displaced reality.

An even more widespread legend in eighteenth- and nineteenth-century France was that of the noble savage. If Chateaubriand could not find any good Quakers in America, certainly he could find some virtuous Indians. But civilization had made its inroads, had debauched the nobility of the original savages, if indeed they had been noble. What Chateaubriand saw, in one of his rare realistic passages concerning the Indians, was filth and squalor: he remarks on the dirty Indian dwellings he has seen. Likewise he speaks of the aspect of American cities as "dull and monotonous" because of the lack of monuments. Finally, the most serious disappointment of all must have been the failure to see George Washington.

IV *Imaginative Invention*

Chateaubriand was disappointed by what he saw; therefore he did precisely what could be expected of one of his imagination: he turned inward and through the years, out of his faded memories, out of his readings, out of his imagination especially, he built a new America which was precisely to his taste. In 1811, in the *Itinerary from Paris to Jerusalem* we find a typical invention of this sort: the episode of M. Violet, the exiled Frenchman in powdered wig who gives dancing lessons to the savages.

When I arrived in the country of the Cayugas, a tribe which was part of the Iroquois nation, my guide led me into a forest. In the center of this forest there was a kind of barn; in this barn I found a score of savages, men and women, smeared with paint like sorcerers, their bodies half nude, their ears cut jagged, raven's feathers on their heads and rings through their noses. A little Frenchman, hair powdered and curled as in the old days, with an apple-green jacket, was scraping away on a pocket-sized violin and was having the Iroquois dance *Madelon Friquet.* M. Violet (that was his name) was dancing-master to the savages. They payed him for their lessons in beaver skins and bear hams: he had been kitchen boy in the service of General Rochambeau during the Revolution. He stayed in New York after the departure of our army, and he decided to teach the fine arts to the Americans. His views having broadened with his success, the new Orpheus carried civilization to the wandering hordes of the New World. In speaking to me of the Indians, he always said "these gentlemen savages and lady savagesses." He boasted much of the adroitness of his students: indeed, I have never seen such jumping. M. Violet, holding his little violin between his chin and his chest, turned the fatal instrument; he cried in Iroquois: "To your places!" And the whole troop jumped about like a band of demons.[6]

Such an extraordinary figure as M. Violet naturally sparked a great deal of controversy. Did Chateaubriand really come across such a person? A minute search of records and journals has been made by American scholars, particularly Professor Morris Bishop, without the slightest bit of supporting evidence being found. M. Violet is an invention, and a typical one. If we look closely at any text of Chateaubriand, we see that his mind invariably worked in contrasts: the ancient world and the modern world, the New World and the Old; it is only to be expected that Chateaubriand would want to find the most dramatic contrasts he could. Surely this confrontation of the state of nature and civilization produces precisely the effect he sought. This is not the only example of such invention; it is merely the most striking. Of those which can be accurately documented, an example is the piano which Chateaubriand describes as being played in the wilderness. Here again there is proof that at that time no piano had as yet been transported so far west as Chateaubriand placed it. Again, poetic necessity takes precedence over truth; a detail is needed to heighten the contrast.

But we can find this invention of a fabulous America long before the *Travels in America* and even before the *Itinerary*, since this unreal America existed already in *Atala*.

In a recent article, Raymond Lebègue has attempted to show how certain Indian legends Chateaubriand had read led to the passage concerning "The Two Floridians" in the *Memoirs*. The legends of which Chateaubriand had read speak of a mythical isle where the women are of unbelievable beauty. This provided the stimulus for Chateaubriand's imagination to conceive of the two ideal Indian women he describes.

Much the same is true in *Atala*. First of all, Chateaubriand took all that he has found of interest in Indian lore and mixed together elements from many tribes and many areas, forming an amalgam which in no way represents reality. He was entirely aware of this, and later in the *Travels in America* he did not hesitate to state this in so many words.

V *Chateaubriand's Esthetic*

In questions of standards of beauty, he was likewise quite aware that indeed everyone is ready to admit in principle that beauty is relative and is not a constant and unchanging idea; but he was equally aware that in attempting to convey a set of emotions to his readers, he must use a standard of beauty which is immediately understandable to them on their terms. Did Chateaubriand find the Indian women he saw ugly? This is highly probable: looking at an American Indian with European eyes could scarcely have produced a reaction of admiration on Chateaubriand's part. Here again one can compare what Chateaubriand was expecting with what he found: engravings of American Indian life were current in Europe starting with the reproductions of John White's famous series of paintings in the sixteenth century. The seventeenth century continued the tradition, and the eighteenth century fairly teemed with Indian portraits and scenes. In almost all cases, the features of the Indians are cast in the European mold. Perhaps the artists were unable to capture what for them were totally foreign characteristics, or perhaps they too were consciously painting in an idiom which was to be understood by the European. In any case, a faithful portrait of an Atala could only be ugly. Therefore Chateaubriand depicts Atala as having alabaster-white skin and long golden hair.

Thus in *Atala* as in the *Travels* and all the American scenes, characters and landscapes do not correspond to an esthetic which attempts to approach reality; rather, the author seeks his effect in an artful juxtaposition of suggestive elements.

In speaking of *Atala,* the novelist Julien Gracq attributed to Chateaubriand's primitive descriptions "the inexhaustible charm of a Rousseau painting." This comparison of the novelist with the painter can be said to mark a turning point in the comprehension of Chateaubriand as an artist. The comparison is particularly useful since in this area at least, art criticism is infinitely more advanced than is literary criticism.

No one will contest the place of Rousseau as one of the great painters. Yet as a representation of surface reality, Rousseau's paintings can only be termed crude and childish. But despite the naïve approach and the primitive technique, the paintings are marvelous creations. In the same way, Chateaubriand gives us a picture which is unreal, distorted, made of disparate elements, but which when viewed in the proper light is, or should be, an unquestioned masterpiece. Just as Rousseau, starting from drawing-book pictures of animals and from enlarged and multiplied representations of common house plants, transmuted it all through his imagination into an artistic marvel, so Chateaubriand could take bits and pieces from everywhere and weld them into an esthetically valid whole.

The two artists were perhaps similar in their intent: each was, no doubt, more or less attempting a representation of reality, but in each case the result was an interpretation of reality which far transcended reality itself. Moreover, the two artists are easily compared for the similarity of their subjects. Both loved lush jungle scenes, exotic landscapes, and wild animals. In fact, it would be easy to find a dozen passages from Chateaubriand which would be magnificently illustrated by paintings of Rousseau: "The Snake Charmer," "Storm in the Forest," "The Repast of the Lion," to name only a few of the most obvious canvases.

Why is this esthetic, which seems so easy to accept in art, so difficult to accept when it is a question of Chateaubriand? Certainly, the force of tradition is very great. Because Chateaubriand has for so long been interpreted on the surface level, it becomes difficult to descend into the depths.

Chateaubriand's type of painting is all the more valid in that it is essentially modern, as much as that term might shock the traditional critic as applied to such an author. Without wanting to push the comparison too far, Chateaubriand is much like Stendhal, who had to wait until fifty years after his death for the majority of critics suddenly to realize that the technique of the modern psychological novel was already highly developed in Stendhal's works. There is this difference, however: Stendhal was simply misunderstood by and incomprehensible to his contemporaries. Chateaubriand, on the other hand, was intelligible to his contemporaries on one level, but he has a much more significant meaning on another level for us.

Perhaps a better comparison is Flaubert. *Madame Bovary*

was appreciated and continues to be so as one of the great novels, neatly placed at the transition point between Realism and Naturalism. This does not however preclude such personal and highly ingenious interpretations as those of the authors of the *nouveau roman*, who find in Flaubert the beginnings of the new novel. One thinks particularly of Nathalie Sarraute and her efforts to trace back the genesis of the new style not to the *Education sentimentale*, which would be more immediately comprehensible but to *Madame Bovary*.

This sort of interpretation necessarily minimizes the conscious role of the artist. This is why it is futile to look into what the author says he was intending to do if we want to arrive at a truly valid judgment of his worth. It is not only the artist's conscious mind that is involved in the production of a work of art, but also, and more important, the subconscious. The work of art is important not so much for what it is but for what it can be. As long as it is capable of inspiring the spectator or the reader with new emotions, it is a living piece of art.

VI *Contemporary Aspects of Chateaubriand's Art*

We have frequently spoken of the modern nature of Chateaubriand's work. The word that comes to mind with Chateaubriand in the modern context is "psychedelic." There are many authors, some with talent, who today are attempting to portray the sensations of the user of narcotics. As one of the earlier attempts, we may recall Kenneth Anger's film *Pleasure Dome*, first brought to widespread attention at the Brussels World's Fair. The attempt is an extremely interesting one in which three separate screens are used. Although for technical reasons the three-screen process is not often used, even in the projection of this particular film (aside from the Brussels presentations, perhaps the only successful public performance was in Berkeley, California), these three screens are an essential part of the effect: at times, the peripheral screens complement the central screen, sometimes they are blank, and sometimes they are showing totally different scenes. It is impossible to look directly at more than one screen at a time, but the spectator is aware of certain sensations caused by these peripherally viewed scenes. In all, there is a profusion of color and of exotic detail of setting and costume.

This is not an attempt to suggest that Chateaubriand had happened upon the formula for LSD and that he was a constant user. Drug-taking in the nineteenth century was certainly not uncommon, especially among poets, but with the best of the poets, and this includes Chateaubriand, the artist through the use of his imagination was able to produce in himself these flights of fancy without having recourse to drugs as a stimulus to the mind.

Any of Chateaubriand's famous descriptive passages can be subjected to this kind of analysis. What we see in the famous jungle scenes, in the descriptions of the Mississippi, the paintings of the Indian ceremonies, is first of all a profusion of color. The young Rimbaud had read Chateaubriand, and the *Bateau ivre* bears the traces of the vividly colored scenes the poet found there. The colors are always intense and in sharp contrast with one another. Just as Chateaubriand loved to contrast ideas, he delighted in contrasting colors.

The details of character, action, and scene are designed to afford a maximum number of exotic elements. Balzac was to employ much the same technique on another level with his endless cataloguing of objects. Here another reference to films is called for. Not to restrict the comparison to the relatively esoteric film experiments of a Kenneth Anger, let us use cinerama as the point of comparison. The principle of the wide screen is that the countless details glimpsed out of the corners of the eyes and not fully seen, since the eyes are focused on the center of the screen, go together with one another to form an illusion of reality unobtainable from the ordinary narrow screen. This is not an abstract theory but a practical observation, as can be discovered by anyone who undergoes the experience.

This cinema technique is rather on a physical level of vision. But what Chateaubriand and Balzac are doing is to present the imagination with such a profusion of color and detail that the artistic reality, almost surreality, is infinitely magnified.

Again, this interpretation would no doubt shock Chateaubriand as it would shock any traditional critic discussing the theories of exoticism among the Romantics. But as is so evident in Chateaubriand's own life, it is not what is that is important, but what appears to be. The power of the imagination is infinitely greater than reality. If it is possible to look into Chateaubriand

and see these things, it is because they are implicitly there.

Only when a work of art is capable of constantly renewing itself in this manner does it continue to live. For too long, critics and readers have been unwilling to look for the hidden treasures Chateaubriand offers and, as a result, are left with the superficial platitudes which are indeed unrewarding.

It is therefore important for the reader to refocus his attention on a misunderstood author. The time has come for a re-evaluation, a complete rethinking of Chateaubriand's America. This sort of opportunity does not often present itself in regard to a major author. We have here perhaps one of the most fruitful fields of potential critical endeavor left to us in early nineteenth-century studies.

CHAPTER 6

The Pamphlets and the Political Writings

I Early Political Involvement

A S we have seen, Chateaubriand led an active political life within the government, at least for a time. However, he did not await his attainment of power to begin his involvement in politics, nor did he forego political activity after his political disgrace. In this, Chateaubriand was typical of many European authors who combined statesmanship and letters: Benjamin Constant, Mme de Staël, George Canning, Martínez de la Sierra, to name but a few of the outstanding examples. Indeed, the turbulent years of the early nineteenth century were a fertile field for sometimes violent political tracts, and Chateaubriand was one of the most prolific contributors to this area of activity. Two of his writings most widely known among his contemporaries were *On Buonaparte and the Bourbons* (1814) and *On Monarchy According to the Charter* (1816). A work of a rather different type was *The Congress of Verona* (1838), in which the author detailed his role (real or exaggerated) in that conference which was to determine the fate of Spain then in the throes of rebellion and revolution. This was a work of documentation, of "history" as Chateaubriand saw it.

The first two pamphlets, however, were works of polemic and persuasion. As can be seen by the titles, the subjects are provocative. The Italianate spelling of Buonaparte indicates immediately that the author was no partisan of the empire. The question of the Charter was likewise one of the most hotly debated subjects of the times. The Charter was the document granted by Louis XVIII on his accession to the throne after the first defeat of Napoleon. It represented thus the principle of limited constitutional monarchy, which in Chateaubriand's mind was the ideal government for France.

This, then, is the theme running through many of Chateaubriand's political writings: unquestioned support of the legitimate

105

constitutional monarch. The advantage of such a principle of
legitimacy as Chateaubriand sees it, is that the king is unquestioned—there can be no doubt as to who the ruler should be.
Chateaubriand will therefore oppose Louis-Philippe while he
had supported Charles X, in spite of the fact that Louis-Philippe
might well have been a much better king in Chateaubriand's
estimation, except for the fact that he has no "legitimate" right
to the throne.

II *The Legitimate Monarchy Principle*

Perhaps this emphasis on legitimacy can be explained by a
theme running through all of Chateaubriand's work, not just
the political tracts. The theme is that of insecurity. The childhood scenes as recounted in the *Memoirs* are filled with such
feelings. The attitude is not surprising in view of the future
author's unorthodox upbringing. But to this predeposition must
be added the violent upheavals of a political nature which, in
the course of some forty years, brought such a rapid succession
of governments that they are the despair of students who try
to remember them all. Chateaubriand was witness to these
upheavals and the chaos which followed, including the many
personal tragedies that befell the Chateaubriand family. Again,
it is not surprising that the subject of stability should be the
concern which for him took precedence over all others.

As we shall see in connection with the Spanish republics,
Chateaubriand was interested in ensuring an orderly transferral
of power upon the advent of a new executive. If a revolution
could break out each time a new king or president was chosen,
then the chance of the heir to the throne possibly being a nin-
compoop was less to be feared than the unrest of a disorderly
transition. It must be remembered also that Chateaubriand still
kept much of the old blind faith in providence: providence has
chosen the person who is to govern.

III *Chateaubriand's Political Personality*

Chateaubriand's political life is criticized often on two counts:
first that he was fickle, second that he was ineffectual. There
is a measure of truth in both accusations. Because of his position
mainly outside of government, Chateaubriand more often than
not found himself a member of the opposition. His approach

was therefore negative. Given the intricacies of French politics, it is easy to appear to be on different sides of a question at different times. For example, Chateaubriand could first oppose Charles X and then defend him. During the reign of Charles X Chateaubriand opposed him for his conservatism and authoritarianism. After the 1830 revolution, he supported the deposed Charles X, but this he did only from the point of view of representing the principle of legitimate monarchy.

To the second charge, being ineffectual, there is also a partial defense. It is true that professional diplomats may sneer at Chateaubriand's qualities as ambassador and minister. And it is certain that he was a failure to the extent that he was unable to muster support for his ideas, he was unable to convince those in power that he was right. At the same time, Chateaubriand was frequently right in what he said concerning given situations. Some of his predictions have proven remarkably accurate. Other assessments of situations which the analyst of today would reject immediately as impossible were still perhaps quite accurate given the times in which Chateaubriand lived, and given, above all, the character of the French nation, which Chateaubriand as a great humanist rather than a politician, was able to grasp fully.

As with the other aspects of Chateaubriand's career, it is impossible to deal with all of them as they deserve.[1] Yet once again, an analysis of only one element can serve as an indication of the career as a whole. We may choose, for example, Chateaubriand's writings on the Spanish war of 1823, a war with which he was closely involved. We shall see here clearly the great insight and at the same time the grave shortcomings of Chateaubriand the statesman.[2]

IV *The Spanish Republics*

Chateaubriand's attitudes toward the Spanish republics deserve to be investigated for a variety of reasons. Not only does such an inquiry throw on the famous author an entirely different light from that afforded by the reading of his well-known fiction and travel works, but also, in his political dealing he evidences certain ideas still current in French foreign-policy thinking. Finally, his analysis of the problems of South America retains even now so much of its validity, and although the solution proposed by the author might be, and indeed was found unacceptable, his evaluation of the situation proved to be entirely accurate.

For those who know Chateaubriand as the fanciful portrayer of the American wilderness in *Atala, René,* and *The Natchez,* the religious apologist of *The Genius of Christianity,* or the intrepid, if somewhat imaginative traveler of the *Travels in America* or the *Itinerary from Paris to Jerusalem,* the portrait of Chateaubriand the level-headed statesman may indeed be a strange one. Yet in fact he played a considerable role in government, as we have seen: he held several posts as ambassador (and would have held others except for the conspiracies of certain groups inimical to the author); further, he was one of the French envoys to the Congress of Verona, where he was responsible for the authorship of many of the most significant French documents presented; and above all, shortly after the Congress, he was entrusted with the French Ministry of Foreign Affairs, a post he was to occupy until after the successful termination of France's expedition into Spain to return the Spanish king to his throne.

Since one of the principal matters concerning the congress, as well as one of the determinants in France's decision to intervene in Spain, was the future status of the South American colonies, which were then attempting to free themselves, it can be easily understood that this matter was one which Chateaubriand considered extremely important and one to which he had devoted much study.

The picture we see of Chateaubriand at the Congress of Verona is not at all that of the young Romantic we might expect. Although he was not the chief of the French mission, he was one of the most important delegates: "M. de Serre [ambassador at Naples] was ignored at the Congress, because of his liberal opinions; I was scarcely any more liked, but I was more feared."[3] He already knew a goodly number of the kings and eminent statesmen in attendance at the congress, and those whom he did not know, or with whom he had had rather strained relations in the past, such as Czar Alexander, were quickly won over. Louis XVIII, although not entirely in sympathy with him, nevertheless accepted to a great extent Chateaubriand's suggestions, as did the Prime Minister Villèle. After Chateaubriand's aim of rescuing Ferdinand of Spain was accomplished, he eschewed all false modesty to state: "After this first sensation of pleasure, I felt a certain legitimate satisfaction: I could admit to myself that in politics I was as worthy as in literature, if I was worth anything at all."[4]

Chateaubriand wrote rather extensively on the Spanish colonies and the Spanish War, but for the most part these writings are neglected today. Although he played a significant role for a few months, he was ousted shortly after the end of the war. Hence, his political writings do not have the historic importance of the papers of a powerful and long-serving foreign minister.

Chateaubriand's principal announcements on the subject are to be found in a kind of postscript to *Travels in America* (1827)[5] and certain other pieces: *The Spanish War* (1823),[6] and *The Congress of Verona*,[7] *The Spanish War of 1823*,[8] and *Negotiations: Spanish Colonies*,[9] all of 1838.

Chateaubriand's plan, at first opposed by the prime minister, but eventually accepted, was this: invade Spain to restore the legitimate (Bourbon) monarchy and transform the erstwhile colonies into independent constitutional monarchies, each headed by a Bourbon prince. It is the reasons behind this plan which deserve consideration, for Chateaubriand had a double plan: this course of action was to benefit France and the former colonies at the same time. The benefit for France is of particular interest because of the parallels which may be drawn between the position of Chateaubriand and that of modern France.

Let us begin by sketching the state of affairs. Spain's South American colonies were in the process of liberation under Simón Bolívar. In Europe, Ferdinand had been driven from the Spanish throne. The situation naturally appeared grave for the French king and the cause of legitimacy; indeed, only seven years had passed since the re-establishment of the legitimate government in France after the defeat of Napoleon. Aside from the natural sympathy of one Bourbon monarch for another, as well as the cause of legitimacy, in the view of many Frenchmen, including Chateaubriand, the situation presented grave commercial dangers. The colonies, although existing in fact as republics, were not yet recognized by the major powers. The politics of recognition created problems. The Latin influence of Spain could no longer be exercised: the countries which had just revolted against the colonial power could scarcely be expected to accept graciously a return to the old sphere of influence. To Chateau-

briand and many other Frenchmen, the solution to the problem
was obvious: replace the Spanish influence by a kind of French
tutelage involving nominal independence, but with close-knit
economic and cultural ties with France.

In fact, however, the situation seemed to be leading in an
entirely different direction. Through the granting of loans and
credits, coupled with trade pacts, England was seeking to draw
the new republics out of the sphere of Latin influence into the
Anglo-Saxon domain. Specifically, Chateaubriand believed that
the British foreign minister George Canning was using the
threat of recognition of the republics as a weapon to restrain
France on the Continent in her attempts to invade Spain for
the purpose of effecting a restoration.[10] In this judgment at
least, French Prime Minister Villèle was in entire accord with
Chateaubriand, as is evidenced by a letter he directed to his
envoy: "England has unmasked herself . . . by the proposition
relative to the Spanish colonies, which she has obviously made
only in order to make it possible later for herself . . . to recognize
all of the colonies which are willing to accord her commercial
advantages."[11]

Against this background, the Congress of Verona was to meet
in an effort to decide the course of action in respect to the
Spanish crisis. Those attending made up a brilliant gathering:
kings, noblemen, politicians. Chateaubriand said modestly: "I
was presented to the Kings: I already knew most of them."[12]

Head of the French delegation was Viscount Montmorency,
French foreign minister, later to become Duke Montmorency
upon the successful completion of the congress. Called upon to
play a major role in the delegation was Chateaubriand, brought
to Verona from his post as ambassador in London.

Chateaubriand was later to write his *Congress of Verona*, in
order, he says, to correct any misconceptions concerning the
French part in the congress. France was not, said he, forced into
the war by the other powers; rather, it was a choice determined
by France alone;[13] once again Villèle's ideas coincided with those
of Chateaubriand: "France being the only country having to
act with its own troops, she alone will be judge of the necessity."[14]
France wished thus to keep in her own hands the power to
begin and direct the course of the possible war, without being
willing to subject herself to the deliberations of any international
group of powers.

In the end, despite certain objections, Chateaubriand's opinions were to prevail, especially on his elevation to the post of foreign minister under Villèle. Chateaubriand was now in a position to put into action his plan as he had stated it at the congress when he replied to the memorandum of the Duke of Wellington: "The court of the Tuileries is most anxious, as is the court of St. James, that Spain adopt measures proper to return peace and prosperity to the continent of America. It is in this sincere desire and in the hope of seeing the authority of His Catholic Majesty reestablished, that the Government of His Most Christian Majesty has also refused the advantages offered to it."[15] The first half of this policy, invasion of Spain, was quickly and successfully accomplished. Chateaubriand was, however, to be turned out before being able to accomplish his second purpose of establishing the monarchies.

Despite the ultimate failure of the project, the logic behind the decisions is fascinating from two points of view, not only as indicating a school of politics still current today, but also as revealing a surprising perspicacity on the part of Chateaubriand as to the problems to be faced by the new republics. The two elements are constantly visible in Chateaubriand's argumentation.

First, in respect to France itself, the Spanish affair was to serve definite ends in foreign policy as well as domestic policy. Chateaubriand found France in a near-desperate situation: ". . . legitimacy was dying for lack of victories after the triumphs of Napoleon, and especially after the diplomatic transaction [the treaties of Vienna] which had dishonored it. The idea of liberty in the mind of the French, who will never understand that liberty very well, will never compensate for the idea of glory, their natural idea."[16] Chateaubriand was ready to play international power politics and run the risk of world conflict in order to re-establish France in her former position of world leadership: "Spain, by placing us in danger, both by her principles and her separation from the kingdom of Louis XIV, seemed to be the real battlefield where we might, with great peril it is true, but with great honor, restore at the same time our political power and our military force."[17]

Chateaubriand finally prevailed, and after a rapid campaign, victory was his. These are his feelings upon receiving the telegram announcing the liberation of King Ferdinand: "The telegram and the hundred-gun salute which announced the deliverance of Ferdinand all but made me ill with joy; not, to be sure, that I attached any personal interest in the rescue of a hateful monarch, not that I thought all was finished; but I was in a veritable transport of joy at the idea that France could be reborn powerful and formidable. . . ."[18]

It is true that here Chateaubriand was writing several years after the events, but his opinions are identical with those expressed at the time, as can be seen in a piece called "The Spanish War," which dates from October 12, 1823: "All was great, noble, chivalrous in the deliverance of Spain. Legitimate France will possess eternally the glory of having stopped the armaments race, and of having been the first to reestablish on the high seas the right of property which was already respected in all wars on land by civilized nations, and the violation of which in marine law is a remains of the piracy of barbarous times."[19] He continues: "our successes in Spain return our homeland to the military rank of the great powers of Europe, and assure our independence."

V *Diplomatic Failures*

The other half of Chateaubriand's program, to establish the Bourbon constitutional monarchies, was less easy to achieve. Precisely at the moment when steps could have been taken in this direction, Chateaubriand was replaced as foreign minister. His pronouncements on the subject therefore take on a kind of bitterness and almost satisfaction in seeing that all was not well in the erstwhile Spanish colonies: "The Spanish colonies formed into constitutional monarchies would have completed their political education sheltered from the storms by which new-born republics can be overturned. History has only too well verified my predictions: in what a state are those colonies today? An eternal civil war, successive tyrants behind the name of liberty."[20]

The reasoning which lay behind these conclusions is to be found at the end of the *Travels in America*. Chateaubriand was naturally led into the subject by his considerations of democracy in America. As was the case with most of his contemporaries, he had not at first been able to conceive of a successful democracy in modern times, thinking only of the ancient manifestations of that form of government. What he read of North America and what he saw there in 1791 led him to revise his ideas:

. . . There are two types of practical liberty. One belongs to the infancy of nations; it is the daughter of manners and virtue—it is that of the first Greeks, the first Romans, and that of the Savages of America. The other is born out of the old age of nations; it is the daughter of enlightenment and reason—it is this liberty of the United States which replaces the liberty of the Indian. Happy land which in the space of less than three centuries has passed from the one liberty to the other almost without effort, and that by a battle which lasted no more than eight years![21]

Chateaubriand had great hopes for American democracy as opposed to the necessary fate of the earlier democracies:

Whatever the future, liberty will never entirely disappear from America; and it is here that we must point out one of the great advantages of liberty, daughter of enlightenment, over liberty, daughter of manners.

Liberty, daughter of manners, disappears where her principle is altered, and it is of the nature of manners to deteriorate with time. Liberty, daughter of manners, begins before despotism in the days of obscurity and poverty; she finally is lost in the centuries of brilliance and luxury. Liberty, daughter of enlightenment, shines after the ages of oppression and corruption; she walks with the principle which preserves and renews her; the enlightenment of which she is the effect, far from weakening with time, as do the manners that give birth to the first liberty, the enlightenment, I say, fortifies itself rather with time; thus it does not abandon the liberty it has produced; always in the company of that liberty, it is at the same time the generative virtue and the inexhaustible source of liberty.[22]

VI *The Future of Democracy in America*

Chateaubriand foresaw, however, friction between North America and the Spanish republics, and at the same time he predicted an internal conflict in the United States over the question of slavery and other questions of local interest which would tend to divide the country.

This discussion led him directly into his considerations on the Spanish republics. After expressing his confidence in American democracy, he exclaims: "I would like to be able to say as much for the Spanish Republics of America. They enjoy independence; they are separated from Europe; it is an accomplished fact, an immense fact no doubt in its results, but a fact that does not immediately and necessarily lead to liberty" (p. 193).

He continues to explain the opposition between the two Americas by citing historical and cultural differences. First, the English colonists were for a great part dissidents who sought refuge. In spite of this, the English institutions had prepared them for self-government: "As Englishmen, the colonists of the United States were already accustomed to a public discussion of the interests of the people, the rights of the citizen, the language and form of constitutional government. They were learned in the arts, letters and sciences; they shared all the enlightenment of their mother country" (p. 194).

In comparison, Chateaubriand finds the Spaniards poorly prepared: "In Old Spain were they educated in the school of liberty? Did they find in their former nation the institutions, teachings, examples, and enlightenment that form a people for constitutional government?" (p. 195). Other difficulties quoted are those of geography: difficult communications, unfavorable climate. But above all, one factor differentiates the two areas, the nature of their revolutions:

The United States rose up on their own accord, tiring of the yoke and loving independence; when they had broken their chains, they found within themselves sufficient enlightenment to guide themselves. . . .

In the Spanish republics the facts are of a quite different nature:

Although miserably administered by the mother country, these colonies moved first rather by the effect of a foreign stimulus than by the instinct of liberty. (p. 197)

It can be seen therefore that the Spanish colonies were not, as were the United States, driven to emancipation by a powerful principle of liberty. . . . A stimulus from without, political interests, and extremely complicated events—that is what is to be seen at first glance. The colonies detached themselves from Spain because Spain was invaded. . . . That is not all; foreign money and speculation tended to deprive them of what might remain of their liberty which was native and national. (p. 198)

Finally, Chateaubriand examines the advantages of the South American countries: "They contain within their vast limits all the elements for prosperity: variety of climate and soil, forests for the navy, ports for the ships, a double ocean which opens to them the commerce of the world. Nature has been prodigal in everything with these republics; everything is rich on and under the land that supports them; the rivers fecundate the surface of the land, and gold fertilizes its breast. Spanish America has therefore before it a propitious future; but telling these countries they can achieve it without effort, would be deceiving them, lulling them into false security: the flatterers of peoples are as dangerous as the flatterers of kings" (p. 200).

Again, he regrets that his solution was not the one adopted. Thus would many of the difficulties have been avoided:

In my opinion, the Spanish Colonies would have gained much by setting themselves up as constitutional monarchies. Representative monarchy is in my estimation a government far superior to the republican government because it destroys individual pretension to the executive power and unites order and liberty.

It also seems to me that representative monarchy would have been more appropriate to the Spanish genius and the actual state of persons and affairs in a land where great landed property dominates, where the number of Europeans is small and that of the Negroes and Indians considerable, where slavery is customary, where the state religion is the Catholic religion, and especially where education is completely lacking in the popular classes. . . . A people suddenly emerging from slavery, rushing into liberty, can fall into anarchy, and anarchy almost always gives birth to despotism. (p. 202)

VII   *Evaluation of Chateaubriand's Views*

This extremely lucid view of the world and its problems is indeed astonishing coming from the pen of Chateaubriand, who after all is best known, and deservedly so, as a primitive painter of the beauties of nature and religion. In the field of politics, many others played roles in government infinitely more important than Chateaubriand. Yet he was able to probe directly to the heart of a problem in international policy and politics, and arrive at an evaluation which history has proved to be only too accurate.

Our own age frowns on the idea of a monarch, even a constitutional one, particularly if imposed from without, and at least most of the world refuses the idea of force as a means to glory. Yet while rejecting Chateaubriand's solutions, we must admit the logic which led him to such decisions, especially in view of the fact that his predictions proved accurate. Finally, in respect to his own age, the solutions he proposed were very possibly far better than those adopted.

From the point of view of the student of literary history, in the last analysis, Chateaubriand the statesman can serve as a fine counterpart to the better-known Chateaubriand of literature, to whom some critics like to attach adjectives such as vain, ridiculous, and untrustworthy.

CHAPTER 7

Works of History and Erudition

I *Relative Interest of these Works*

CERTAINLY this is the portion of Chateaubriand's work which has retained the least interest for the general public, and whose importance even for the scholars is purely relative. This is not to say that these works have not yielded valuable insights into the mind and method of the author; these insights in turn serve to give greater illumination to the work as a whole.

The first of Chateaubriand's books to fit into this category is also his first published work, *Historical, Political and Moral Essay on Ancient and Modern Revolutions, Considered in Their Relation to the French Revolution.* The *Essay* appeared in 1797, the fruit of Chateaubriand's labors during his English exile. Although the eventual aim of the work was to underline the repetitive nature of history and the similarity of the circumstances underlying all revolutions, the detail of the work is as heteroclite as any of the ones to follow. Reminiscences of American scenes alternate with ideas inspired by readings of multitudes of authors, ancient and modern.

Three main sources of interest are to be found in the *Essay*. First, there are certain pages, particularly those describing America, which rank among the greatest anthology pages: there is already an unmistakable mastery of style and image. Second, from the point of view of the author's intellectual development, the work allows us to assess the degree to which the young man was still under the enormous influence of the eighteenth-century French *philosophes*, an influence which in many ways was to disappear from the subsequent work.[1] Finally, the *Essay* allows a first glimpse of a method of composition which will become characteristic of the author. Starting from an extremely varied corpus of notes taken from his readings, he rearranges the materials, interpreting them and embellishing them in his own manner. As was to be the case with so many of his subsequent works,

117

the finished product left much to be desired both on the level of accuracy and on the level of solid logic.

Again, were the work to have been without sequel, it would certainly not deserve the attention of today's reader. Since it is a work of Chateaubriand's apprenticeship, however, it takes on a kind of peripheral interest.

Such is not the case with *The Genius of Christianity*, however. Although in composition and development it is very similar to the *Essay*, its literary and historical interest is enormous. For that reason it has been examined in a separate chapter (Chapter 3).

To an even greater extent, *The Four Stuarts*, published in 1828, can be left with the most rapid treatment. There is perhaps in this work an indication of Chateaubriand's continuing interest in what was to become in the hands of other authors the historical novel, as was seen in the case of *The Natchez*. Indeed, many of the historical scenes presented are obviously the work of the imagination, liberated to wander through a historical setting rather than being bound by the results of patient research and careful logic. One critic characterizes the history well by calling it "a mixture of narrations, portraits, tableaux and reflections which are not always very much in harmony with one another."[2]

Only three years later another historical work appeared, or rather two works published together, *Historical Discourses or Studies on the Fall of the Roman Empire*. This was followed by the *Detailed Analysis of the History of France*. The two works embrace, in a rather strange way, the first the ancient history, the second the modern history of France. Apparently, much of the work was begun as early as 1814, but even in 1831 it does not seem to have reached its final form. There are omissions, and the *Detailed Analysis* in particular seems only to be the plan of a future work. In the introduction, he paints the relentless series of political events that have disrupted his tranquillity; an added deterrent to perfection was the unrelenting pressure of work. Perhaps, in desperation, he published the volumes, seeing no possibility of finishing them. Perhaps also, financial needs drove him to publish at that particular moment. At any rate, the work as we possess it is highly unsatisfactory. There are endless criticisms to be made, and yet there are undeniable qualities. One can see in the *Historical Studies* the same ability to seize a detail and transmit it to the reader in the most vivid way—as in the major works, portraits of indiivduals, sketching of events in broad strokes, and the like. Without these qualities, the work could be dismissed very rapidly indeed. The qualities, however, cause the reader to hesitate and look more deeply; his investigation is to a great extent rewarded by these "gems" of portraiture and interpretation which are to be found there.

II *English Literature*

The *Essay on English Literature* is to an extent also a work of circumstance. It appeared in 1836 as a companion volume to Chateaubriand's translation of Milton's *Paradise Lost*. An early example of the "tie-in sale," it was obviously felt that the two works presented together would encourage the sale above that which could be expected for an individual volume. As had been the case with other works, Chateaubriand already had a point of departure: a series of articles on English Literature had appeared in the well-known periodical the *Mercure* early in the century. These he took up and reworked for the new volume. Also, he had described medieval French literature in detail in the *Historical Studies*. Since to all intents and purposes French and English literature were not separable in those days, the literary language of England still being the Anglo-Norman version of French, Chateaubriand conveniently transferred this entire development to his new book. The rest of the study was completed from Chateaubriand's entensive readings, both of the critical texts and of the literary texts themselves.

Here too, the volume serves admirably to illustrate the manner in which Chateaubriand composed. However, from the point of view of reliable information about English literature, or of outstanding literary merit in work itself, *The Essay on English Literature* leaves much to be desired. The main interest of the work today is in giving the point of view of a nineteenth-century Frenchman interpreting the literature from the other side of the Channel. Frequently these opinions seem peculiar today; even so, they give an initiation into the esthetics of Chateaubriand, as in this discussion of the corruption in art which is due to the writings of Shakespeare:

The universality of Shakespeare, by the authority of the example and the abuse of imitation, has served to corrupt art; it established the error on which the new dramatic school has been founded. If, to reach the heights of the tragic art it suffices to heap together disparate scenes which are without order and without connection, to brew together the burlesque and the tragic, to place the water carrier next to the monarch, the herb-seller next to the Queen, who cannot easily flatter himself as being the equal of the great masters?[3] Anyone at all will take the trouble to retrace the incidents of his day, his conversations with all and sundry, the various things that have come into his sight, the ball and the funeral, the parties of the rich and the distress of the poor; anyone at all who has written his diary hour by hour can write a play in the style of the English poet.

Let us be aware that writing is an art; that this art has its genres; that each genre has its rules. The genres and the rules are not arbitrary; they are born out of nature herself: art has simply separated what nature has jumbled together; it has chosen the most comely features without destroying the resemblance with the model. Perfection does not destroy truth: Racine in all the excellence of his *art*, is more *natural* than Shakespeare, as an *Apollo*, in all his *divinity*, has more *human* form than an Egyptian colossus.[4]

To be sure, the above passage does very little to enlighten us on the nature of Shakespeare's excellence. But at the same time, the passage is extremely enlightening as to Chateaubriand's attitudes and those of his times. Chateaubriand is writing in the midst of the controversy between the Romantics and the traditionalists in drama. Victor Hugo is tearing down the walls of compartmentalization and opening the theater to liberty. But this contrasts sharply with Chateaubriand's esthetics. The lessons learned from such passages as these can be easily applied to the author's works of high literary value in order to explain the exact nature of these works, the precise form they have attained.

This, in general, is the value of these secondary works: they offer us a mine of information which, when applied to the major works, provide an insight that would be difficult to obtain otherwise. *Atala* and *René* take on an added dimension when they are analyzed in this kind of light.

CHAPTER 8

Penance: The Life of Rancé

I *Inspiration for the Work*

TOWARD the end of Chateaubriand's career, the thought of death quite naturally began to occupy him. Past seventy-five, the subject would under any circumstances be a normal one, but it was made even more oppressive by the pall of death that had constantly surrounded him not only during the revolution, but even during the empire and later. His own family was involved in many of these losses: both family and friends had mounted the scaffold. Others fell victim to political intrigue. One can only speculate as to the effect there must have been on Chateaubriand also when the impatient directors of the corporation holding the rights to Chateaubriand's *Memoirs* ill concealed their hopes for the author's death, anxious for the posthumous publication to begin.

It was in this framework that the idea of the *Life of Rancé* was presented to him. This idea came at the suggestion of the Abbé Seguin, a close moral adviser to Chateaubriand in these later year, and the good abbé proposed as an act of penance that Chateaubriand write the history of the life of Rancé, the celebrated reformer of the Trappist order in France in the seventeenth century.

Seguin could scarcely have foreseen what his simple suggestion would give rise to, for in Chateaubriand's hands the work was to be no simple hagiography. Indeed, the life of Rancé was to be merely the suggestion, the point of departure, which was to give rise to a work of literature completely transcending the subject and totally different from what could be expected under ordinary circumstances.

Indeed, the bare materials of Rancé's biography were bizarre enough to tempt Chateaubriand immediately. Rancé began as one of those society clerics whose number was legion in the

121

seventeenth century. More or less committed to religious vows, still they indulged in all sorts of socio-religious activity which ranged all the way from the direction of the consciences of great ladies of society to careers in literature and occupations in the secular social domain. Rancé was the ardent admirer of Mme de Montbazon, one of the most brilliant leaders of this society. Her sudden death so affected Rancé that he underwent a great moral conversion. He left the world of society and devoted the rest of his life to turning the Trappist order of monks back to their original extreme austerity.

One portion of the Rancé story, perhaps apocryphal, but which nonetheless greatly attracted Chateaubriand, was this: when Rancé came to view the body of Mme de Montbazon, he discovered that apparently the casket had been too short for the body; so the head had been cut off to make the body fit. Rancé took the head and forever after kept the skull of his beloved on his worktable at the monastery. The legend was further popularized by the painting of the celebrated Hyacinthe Rigaud whose portrait of Rancé seated at his work table before the skull of Mme de Montbazon is such a vivid portrayal of the vanity of life and the ever-presence of death.

But Chateaubriand's work transcends this frequently melodramatic subject matter, becoming an infinitely extended meditation on death, couched in what is perhaps the most perfect of stylistic expressions to come from the pen of this master of style.

In some ways, the work is very similar to the previous ones. As in so many other cases, Chateaubriand began with a study of all the writings of and about Rancé. Just as he voraciously read all the travel books about America before setting off on his journeys, and just as he used massive portions of these readings in developing his book of travels, he carefully read and excerpted all that was of interest concerning Rancé. These fragments of reading form an important part of his text.

The exact manner of utilization of these texts provides an important contrast with the earlier works, however. In earlier times, he was careful to integrate these materials into his text to the point that it was usually not apparent, certainly not obvious, that he was using material of others. Everything was consumed, digested, and re-formed before it served its purpose in the book. Here, however, there is a constant and obvious use of quotation which is meant to present the theme on which Chateaubriand will compose variations. There is a constant counterpoint of Chateaubriand's comments which underlies the materials drawn from the earlier writers. This device of constant quotation has another purpose: one of the major aims of Chateaubriand here is stylistic. By the juxtaposition of many contrasting styles of different authors, placed next to his own ever-changing style, he creates a pattern which is truly impressive.

There are four main parts to the work. Book I paints the early life of Rancé and his role in society. Book II shows him undertaking his reform of the Trappist order, together with his trip to Rome and his confrontation with papal authorities. Book III is a kind of *Vita nuova* in which all the rigor of the new reforms becomes apparent. Book IV finally paints the declining years.

II *Stylistic Elements*

To tell this story, Chateaubriand has purposely adopted an appropriate framework. He tells the tale in the same manner as did the seventeenth-century masters of prose in their relations. The temptation to compare Chateaubriand with such seventeenth-century novelists as Mme de La Fayette is constant. This style is beautifully suited to the subject he is treating but it is only the framework. This smooth-flowing, even form of narration, almost neutral in its color, serves only to create a startling contrast with the intrusive elements.

Perhaps more than any other work of Chateaubriand, *Rancé* has evoked interest for the modern reader and critic to an extent not at all to be predicted from the reaction of the contemporaries when the work was first published. A host of modern novelists and critics have heaped praise on it, and the relatively large number of modern editions of the work available today gives testimony to the interest of the public.[1] A few of the comments of the critics, and particularly the novelists, may start us on the path to a clearer understanding of the nature of the work.

III *Modern Appreciation of the Work: Gracq and Jouhandeau*

Julien Gracq, whose tasteful appreciation of Chateaubriand's nature painting has already been seen (see Chapter 5) makes a

most appropriate use of Chateaubriand and the *Life of Rancé*
in his novel *Un beau ténébreux*. In a surrealist setting we see
only dimly the character of the central figure, but we are constantly aware of an aura of death. It is quite logical then, to
find the *Life of Rancé* playing an important role. Here is the
reaction of the narrator on reading the work:

Read Chateaubriand's *Life of Rancé* recently,—no doubt inspired by
that instinctive power of divination which always leads me to the book
which is most singularly prepared to suit my humor. An astonishing
book, abruptly *griffonné* [scribbled],[2] I mean drawn by the careless,
fabled claw of the griffon, that monster with claws of lightning who
is the born writer. Ramified, hairy, ominous, it is like the burnt
branching of grey ash left after lightning has struck. It has the taste
of ashes on Ash Wednesday, the astringent force of the cold, lucid,
barren September mornings which seem suddenly to empty out the
planet with the crisp noises of lofts and wine-presses, and which seem
suddenly to turn the world into the apartment after the moving men
have come, and where the footsteps echo. Then there is the feeling
of riding full speed through apartments furnished with phantoms,
attics of dreams where shimmer sequined dresses, crinolines, yellowed
but incomparable lace, doublets, aigrettes,—with the clacking noise
of a skeleton team—with the rapid movement of a spectral farandole
evoked by Molière's *Don Juan*. From time to time an acrid sentence,
shaking off the illusion, with the taste of a dead leaf long ago spat
out onto a vine denuded by the vintage, chews the cud of bitterness
like an old horse. . . .
You seem to hear sly steps in this book, cleared out by great
shovelfuls as in the cemetery in *Hamlet*—where the echoes become
broader, more crystalline, as in a long succession of empty rooms,
where you hear for a long time the crackling of dry twigs underfoot
on the frozen paths of winter. Something is approaching: what a
surprise! It is Death? It is only death.
A book entirely made up of harmonics, like an exhausted harp which
only hums by a kind of sluggish sympathetic resonance, half frozen,
dulled. It is indeed the most pathetic *Nunc dimittis* of all our
literature.[3]

Gracq's sustained imagery of memories likened to pieces of
furniture to be moved in and out of rooms and attics is particularly appropriate to *Rancé*. For Chateaubriand, too, the elements of memory have this fascinating mobility which allows
them to move back and forth, up and down, attaching themselves
to all sorts of new situations and forming new associations.

A startlingly similar impression of the work comes from another distinguished contemporary novelist, Marcel Jouhandeau. In the book he sees

. . . a marvelous catch-all of treasures into which a genius has emptied his pockets before leaving us. The virtually universal experience of the author allows him to sound the depths of the abyss and measure the height of the summit, the infinities of on high and down below, without ever being artificial in either place.[4]

Later in this same introduction, where Jouhandeau so clearly delineates the startling qualities of *Rancé*, he declares:

The Life of Rancé is a repertory of all possible styles, all tones, all scales, all possible combinations of words; everything that the language can afford in the way of expression is represented here, as in a theatrical prop-room, from simplicity to majesty, from familiarity to the sublime, and each example is straight away carried to perfection, to the universal, without pretension, without the fact even being realized, with the greatest virtuosity, with a royal detachment. (p. 12)

Here too the extreme mobility of the elements of memory is emphasized. Once again it is not necessarily the constituent parts of the book which are of interest, but rather the way in which they are fitted together, then disjoined to be assembled again in another pattern. The principle is precisely that of a kaleidoscope, where a relatively few basic patterns are shifted by the rotation of the tube into a magnificent display of ever-changing visual effects.

IV *Particular and Personal Aspects of the Work*

One of the charms of Chateaubriand's text is the constant series of literary asides, what one might today call "in-jokes," which are destined to carry on a light banter with the reader on a level of wit and sarcasm. For example, when Chateaubriand had cause to mention Rancé's involvement with the society of that most famous of all French letter writers, Mme de Sévigné, he cannot keep from referring to her as "Mme de Sévigné, too many of whose letters were perhaps published . . ." (p. 95). Likewise, he refers to the cardinal de Retz as the "old mitred acrobat" (p. 95).

Occasionally in one of these literary asides, Chateaubriand paints a breathtaking thumbnail portrait. Pascal, whose delineation of what he called the "spirit of finesse" and the "spirit of geometry" has become one of the most celebrated concepts, is the subject of one such sketch. "The terrible Pascal, haunted by his spirit of geometry, was in continual doubt: he escaped from his misery only by plunging into faith" (p. 115). This is the type of remark which caused a Jouhandeau to exclaim on the universal experience of Chateaubriand which allows him such unparalleled perspective.

These asides are not always literary. They frequently are personal, to the point of moving the reader strongly through the presentation of an event, an anecdote, or an emotion from the author's own life. These digressions are always motivated by a rather complicated system of association of ideas. Thus, his discussion of the chateau of Chambord leads him to muse on the efforts that had been made in Chateaubriand's time to return the chateau to Henri, count of Chambord, heir to the throne. This in turn recalls to Chateaubriand his recent trip to London to see the count; this in succession, through rather Proustian identity of place which closely associates two far distant points in time, evokes simultaneously the glorious days as ambassador and the early revolutionary days when Chateaubriand, a penniless refugee, was living in London:

That orphan [the count of Chambord] recently summoned me to London; I obeyed this closed book of misfortune. Henri offered me his hospitality on land slipping away from under his feet. I revisited that city, the scene of my brief grandeur and my interminable misery, I revisited the squares filled with fog and silence, from which there emerged the phantoms of my youth. How much time has passed already since the day when I dreamt of René in Kensington up to these last hours! The old exile found himself charged with showing the orphan a city that my eyes could scarcely recognize. (p. 68)

Chateaubriand's frequent descriptive passages concerning the sites he is presenting are equally mingled with personal impressions and references. He goes to visit the Trappist house:

The Abbey had not been moved: it was still, as at the time of its foundation, located in a valley. The hills assembled around it hid it from the rest of the earth. I felt, in seeing it, that I was once more looking at my woods and my ponds of Combourg in the evening amidst the heavy rays of sunlight. Silence reigned: if there was a noise to be heard, it was only the sound of the trees or the murmurs of some stream; weak or swollen according to the slightness or the rapidity of the wind; one could not be certain it was not the sound of the sea. Only at the Escorial have I encountered such an absence of life: the masterpieces of Raphael stared at one another in the somber sacristies: only the voice of a passing foreigner was barely audible. (pp. 104-5)

Above all, it is Chateaubriand's gift for expression which sets the *Life of Rancé* apart from other works. It is necessary to read the text slowly, savoring each sharp detail. Two of the most famous figures in French history are the cardinals Mazarin and de Retz. One would expect everything that could have been said of them to be long since done. Yet Chateaubriand finds the perfect way to characterize them. Of Mazarin he says:

He braved the storms, wrapped in Roman purple: forced to withdraw in the face of public hatred, he returned through the faithful passion of a woman, leading Louis XIV by the hand. (p. 96)

The reference is, of course, to Ann of Austria, mother of Louis XIV, and regent during her son's minority.

Retz is less well treated by Chateaubriand, being referred to as "an old broken alarm clock." He continues:

Reduced to himself and placed outside the arena of events, he showed himself to be inoffensive: not that he had undergone one of those metamorphoses which are the forerunners of the last leave-taking, but because he had that faculty of changing form which belongs to certain poisonous beetles. Lacking a moral sense, in this lack he found his strength. (p. 96)

Of the *Memoirs* of the cardinal de Retz, Chateaubriand says: "After exhuming him from his *Memoirs,* they found a body buried alive which had devoured itself inside the coffin" (p. 97).

Such expressions are electric. They force the reader to stop and marvel at their brilliance. They suggest reflections which are forever renewing themselves.

French literature, perhaps more than many others, has a tradition of the literary work which lives by its brilliance of expression rather than by any other quality. To a certain extent, the success of such a work depends on the willingness of the reader to seek out and appreciate such a recondite kind of esthetic pleasure. Certainly, as with *Atala,* the temptation to misread the work is ever-present. Just as the reader expecting that *Atala* will reveal to him the faithful picture of primitive

Indian life in America is bound to be disappointed, so the reader who approaches *Rancé* for the history of a saint's life is bound to be dismayed.

An exercise in the brilliance of style, a tour de force of varied expression, a collection of verbal jewels contrived from ill-assorted and uneven stones, but which put together by the hands of a master form a dazzling cascade of pure light: these are the characteristics of the *Life of Rancé*.

CHAPTER 9

Memoirs from Beyond the Grave

I *Chateaubriand's Masterpiece*

THERE is almost universal agreement today that if one work of Chateaubriand is to be singled out as the masterpiece, that work is the *Memoirs.* This was not the immediate reaction to the work's publication, as many of the first readers were frankly disappointed, and this disappointment was perhaps underscored by the rather petty actions of certain critics whose personal jealousies may have clouded their judgment.

With the passage of time, however, and especially after the almost mystical period of fifty years, which so often provides new perspectives on controversial authors, the work began to assume its proper position in the literary world. This period of a half-century seems somehow to have served as a buffer between the opinions of Chateaubriand's contemporaries, too close to the author to have real perspective, and the later critics to whom the dimension of time had given greater clairvoyance.

Just why Chateaubriand's *Memoirs* are his masterpiece is difficult to define; it is much easier to catalogue the work's faults. In the book, Chateaubriand is completely lacking in accuracy: at times he is even incapable of remembering his correct birthday; he is even more uncertain of the year of birth of his favorite sister, Lucile; facts are misstated or deformed; and the account of events is highly partisan.

All these faults seem to fade in importance, however, in the face of the enormous interest the book maintains for the reader of today. Stated as simply as possible, Chateaubriand was a master of words. Irrespective of his subject matter, he could create a flood of narrative and description that have not been rivaled. But beyond that, the *Memoirs* are filled with fascinating subject matter to heighten even more the fascination of Chateaubriand's writing.

The subject of any memoirs is obviously the author himself

and his times. It would be difficult to find a more colorful figure
than Chateaubriand: a giant of the literary world of his time,
but equally involved in the political life of a nation during some
of its most turbulent years. Chateaubriand knew everyone from
the Czar of all the Russias to Mme Récamier, one of the most
beguiling women of French society. To be sure, it would be
foolhardy to use the *Memoirs* as source material for a scientific
study, but scientific exactness is not the province of memoirs.
They are of necessity extremely personal, and their value lies
precisely in the fact that everything is seen refracted through
the eyes of the author.

As in all of Chateaubriand's works, there can be seen here the
incredible ability the author has to keep a whole universe in
his mind. When he thinks of America, his mind is immediately
filled with the similarities and contrasts afforded by the history
of the Old World—all is ordered around vast comparisons on
a massive scale. This technique is the ideal material of memoirs,
and indeed it is an entire society, an entire world, that is pictured in the work. Chateaubriand's whole life, with its literary,
social, and political associations, is distilled into the narrative.
Chateaubriand's merit lies, therefore, in a combination of stylistic
mastery and fascinating subject matter.

II *Circumstances of Composition and Publication*

One of the reasons for the superiority of this work over all
the others is the fact that it occupied the author for a period
of almost forty-five years. The first ideas for the *Memoirs of
My Life,* as he then referred to the work, go back to the early
years of the nineteenth century. Not only was a great deal of
time spent on the composition, but infinite care was taken in
revising and rewriting. There are two processes at work here.
First of all, much of what Chateaubriand wrote during his
career was in effect only a rough draft of the materials for his
Memoirs—the *Travels in America,* the Histories, the *Essay on
English Literature,* and so on, were to reappear as much as
twenty years later in the *Memoirs.* A remarkable perspective can
be obtained when an author is constantly revising things he
had written so long before. But even after the materials had
entered into the manuscript of the *Memoirs,* they continued to
undergo change. There were countless sessions at which Chateau-

briand read portions of his memoirs to close friends. The duchess
de Duras, herself an author of great talent and intelligence,
counseled Chateaubriand at first, but later on, and to a much
greater extent, Mme Récamier was the sounding board for the
author's ideas. It was in Mme Récamier's fashionable salon and
before a very select elite that many of the readings were done.
Mme de Chateaubriand herself exerted a certain amount of
influence on the elaboration of the *Memoirs*.

A good description of the readings of the *Memoirs* in Mme
Récamier's salon exists. It comes from the first volume of
Chateaubriand's *Complete Works* as published by Pourrat in
1837. The entire first Volume consists of an anonymous "Essay
on the Life and the Works of M. de Chateaubriand." Although
no name of an author is given, it is easy to see Chateaubriand
himself behind this essay. Here is the description of the reading
sessions:

> You may then understand France's emotion upon learning that M.
> de Chateaubriand had just given a confidential reading of the
> *Memoirs of His Life*, to a small number of the elect. . . . The little
> salon of l'Abbaye-aux-Bois brightly lit, its mysterious door opening
> only to a few known voices, the windows half-shuttered by the flower-
> ing jasmine. A calm and soothing retreat, at the same time social and
> holy, noisy and silent, an asylum of beauty where comes to rest the
> greatest genius of this century, filled with the noblest of passions and
> author of the most illustrious of works. Imagine an elite gathering
> straining to hear these pages read in the same voice that dictated
> them, and which they alone will hear in this cool and softly-lit salon,
> facing Gérard's Corinne[1] and presided over by that woman,[2] still so
> bright-eyed, with such a calm and tranquil smile. Then finally the
> great poet of our age, the illustrious father of René, Chactas, Atala,
> Eudore, Velléda, Cymodocée, all the fancies, all the enthusiams, all
> the faith, all the poetry of our age, opening with a steady hand those
> immortal pages which will see the light of day only after his death.
> —That so soft and vibrant voice reciting, the way conscience speaks,
> all the phases of that life which was so exemplary by its virtue, work
> and genius. —Indeed that was enough to whet the appetites of those
> passionate and attentive listeners; indeed that was sufficient cause
> for listening intently in a kind of holy meditation.[3]

Obviously the scene is greatly exaggerated, and yet it is only
in such exaggeration that we can sense the kind of cult that
surrounded Chateaubriand and especially the *Memoirs*.

A great any pages of manuscript of the *Memoirs* are in existence, partly because of the financial arrangements, which will be discussed in a moment, but also because of Chateaubriand's work habits. Some of the manuscripts were written by Chateaubriand himself, occasionally by Mme de Chateaubriand, but usually a secretary was used. The manuscript would then be put aside, to be taken up again at a later date. Then Chateaubriand set about replacing words, crossing out sentences, adding new paragraphs, sometimes filling the margins completely with tiny cramped writing, very unlike his usual very tall, spaced hand. The secretary would then take the manuscript and recopy it, incorporating the corrections. Then Chateaubriand would take up the new manuscript again and perhaps once more cover it with corrections. Parts of the manuscript originally written in 1811 were still being revised and annotated in the 1830's and 1840's. Almost all the earlier manuscripts were destroyed, but enough material survived to reveal the infinite care and patience that went into the revisions.

The *Memoirs* were always meant for posthumous publication, and Chateaubriand early decided on the title *Memoirs from Beyond the Grave*. It is clear that the author would have preferred a waiting time of fifty years after his death before the work was published, but circumstances were to force another course of action. In any case, it is certain Chateaubriand wanted to feel completely free to say whatever he wanted in his *Memoirs* without having to worry about practical considerations of hurt feelings and personal vendettas. The *Memoirs* may seem not very tendentious or controversial to the reader of today, but to the reader of 1850 they at times almost approached the level of scandal since they frequently involved the foibles of the great and the near-great.

Chateaubriand, however, suffered from the ill of all younger sons of the not-too-rich nobility—lack of money. Traditionally younger sons had careers in the army or the church, and we have seen that Chateaubriand started out on an army career, but the revolution intervened. Chateaubriand could have done as many did and serve first Napoleon, then Louis XVIII, then Charles X, then Louis-Philippe, but Chateaubriand was a man of principle and given to grandiose gestures which were often harmful to him personally. His open denunciation of Napoleon ended a career with the empire. His wounded pride would not

let him accept minor posts under Louis XVIII after his fall from
grace as foreign minister. His vociferous support for the principle
of legitimate monarchy cost him the coveted post of ambassador
to Sweden (the new king of Sweden was Napoleon's General
Bernadotte, an elected monarch, therefore touchy on the subject
of legitimacy). Out of principle, Chateaubriand opposed Charles
X for his reactionary attitudes and then completely disavowed
Louis-Philippe since he did not represent legitimate monarchy.
Mme de Chateaubriand's fortune, it will be remembered, was all
in church investments confiscated during the revolution.

All this meant that a great deal of the time Chateaubriand had
to live by his writings. This is a difficult occupation at any time,
but particularly so in those days when there was no protection
for the author's property. As soon as a book was published in
Paris it was pirated in Brussels. The Brussels edition sold for
less because the author was paid nothing. Ironically, a famous
copy of Chateaubriand's *Memoirs*, the one annotated by the
well-known critic Sainte-Beuve, is not the Paris edition but the
pirated Brussels edition.

The result was that Chateaubriand was often extremely hard-
pressed for money. In a moment of such difficulty he hit upon
a means of preserving his artistic integrity and at the same
time realizing a profit from his *Memoirs*. A corporation was
formed and stock was sold. The corporation was to hold a copy
of the manuscript of the *Memoirs*, this forming the assets of the
corporation. On Chateaubriand's death, the copy he had held,
and had continued to revise, would serve as the basis for the
posthumous publication.

Chateaubriand and his friends showed themselves to be good
businessmen. Through various devices, interest in the *Memoirs*
was kept at a very high level. Chateaubriand mentioned the
Memoirs frequently in his writings, and from time to time published extracts from the work. The readings of the manuscript
at Mme Récamier's salon were carefully reported in the press.
The interest grew to such a point that Chateaubriand frequently
exclaimed that he felt the stockholders in the corporation were
impatient for him to die.

The arrangement worked, however, and a yearly pension was
paid the author by the corporation. When finally in 1848, approaching his eightieth birthday, he died, plans for publication

were immediately put into action, but the task was so monumental a one that it was not completed until 1850.

Incredibly, for the first one hundred years, the work was represented only by an imperfect text. Parts of the manuscript had been lost or stolen. Other parts were removed by Chateaubriand at the last moment as being too personal (the books on Mme Récamier, for example), and still more passages were deleted by the literary executors for a variety of reasons. Finally, for the purposes of publication in installments in a newspaper, the *Memoirs* lost their basic structural division into parts and books, retaining only the chapters.

It was not until 1948 saw the Centenary edition of the *Memoirs* that the work was published in its entirety, thanks to the enormous erudition of the editor, Sorbonne Professor Maurice Levaillant.[4] Even in its imperfect form, the work had gained an ever-increasing following. Since the Centenary edition, readership has grown enormously. Three major subsequent editions have appeared, including a popular paperback in the Livre de Poche series, even further proof of the enormously expanded readership of the *Memoirs*.

III *Physical Aspect of the Work*

To attempt to outline the contents of the *Memoirs from Beyond the Grave* would require the retelling of Chateaubriand's life along with a great deal of French history. This is best left to Chateaubriand, and an actual reading of the text, even a small part of it, will better serve the purpose. Some description of the text will not be amiss, however.

The work is composed of four parts, divided into forty-four books; each book is further broken down into a number of short chapters. Chateaubriand starts with a history of his ancient family, gradually bringing the narrative down to his immediate forebears. He details the birth of his brothers and sisters and finally his own entrance into the world. Nature realized the great event that was taking place that night—there was a terrific storm which was almost without equal in the history of Saint-Malo. The author does not fail to chronicle this event of great portent.

In view of the frequently imaginative nature of the *Memoirs*, one is immediately tempted to suspect a fabrication, especially since there is an obvious literary reminiscence of which Chateaubriand was definitely aware, since he had quoted it in the *Abencerraje*. There he had presented the old Spanish romance of Abenamar "the day you were born there were great portents." But in this particular instance, thanks to the patient scholarship of a critic, it appears that Chateaubriand is dealing with the actual truth: that night there was a great storm in Saint-Malo.

This incident is worth remarking on, because the temptation with Chateaubriand is to reject as fanciful all of the romanesque elements he includes in the *Memoirs*. Of course, these events are frequently fabrications, but occasionally one of these unbelievable events turns out to be quite factual. Once again, we have an example of the way in which Chateaubriand worked. He started with a certain number of facts, of events, of literary sources; then, through his boundless imagination, he created innumerable parallel scenes by analogy with the actual ones.

Chateaubriand then treats his youth, the trip to America, his return and exile, his government posts with the Napoleonic government and then under the restoration, including his return to England as ambassador, which offers ample opportunity for Chateaubriand's predilections for vast comparisons, by allowing him to contrast the penniless exile of his first stay in England, with the magnificent return as the representative of His Most Christian Majesty.

The recitals of Chateaubriand's many travels, the portraits of all the great and near-great personages he meets, make of this part of the narrative a vast painting of the period. The ensuing years of political activity broaden the horizons of the *Memoirs* to include all the great events of that period's history. In the later years of his life, Chateaubriand was often embittered and unhappy. This state of mind colored these last years as seen through the *Memoirs*.

To all intents and purposes, the *Memoirs* were complete around 1846, two years before the author's death. He kept his personal copy of the manuscript, of course, and frequently reviewed and slightly revised certain portions, but the bulk of the work was complete. The manuscript was kept in a chest at the foot of his simple iron bed. It was still there on July 4, 1848, when the author died. This physical association of the man and his work until the very end has an almost mystical quality about it—one is tempted to say that the spirit passed

out of the man and into the manuscript, endowing it with
eternal life.

IV *The Nature of the Memoirs*

Several parts of the *Memoirs* deserve particular attention, and
they may be used as an indication of the nature of the whole.
Moreover, much of what has been said concerning the earlier
works may be deemed completely applicable here. For example,
the entire episode of the trip to America finds its place in the
Memoirs. All that has been said in Capter 5 about Chateaubriand's poetic vision of America is equally germane here. Likewise, much of what was said of the Romantic character of the
hero of *René* is important in relation to the fanciful portrait of
Chateaubriand's youth that we find in the opening pages of the
Memoirs, for the portrait we see in the *Memoirs* is in many
ways just as fanciful as the picture of René: the *Memoirs* contain
much more psychological truth than literal truth.

Before entering into the detail of the *Memoirs*, three broad
facets of the work must be examined, all concerned with form.
First, memoirs are a very particular type of book, resembling
at the same time history and the novel, even poetry perhaps.
Second is the question of tone, an exceedingly important concern
for Chateaubriand. Finally is the matter of technique. Each one
of these broad facets embodies certain inherent vices, but it is
perhaps to a large extent as a result of these concerns that the
book was to become the masterpiece it is.

What are memoirs? They are personal history, a partisan view
of events and times, as seen through the eyes of one of the
principal actors. With Chateaubriand, however, the technique
of memoirs goes far beyond this to become an even more personal
document. A good evaluation of what the *Memoirs* are, is to be
found in the already mentioned biographical introduction to the
Pourrat edition of the *Complete Works*. Part of the publicity
campaign, the *Memoirs* are mentioned prominently, with an
acute evaluation of their nature, which could only have been
supplied by Chateaubriand himself:

But were these *Memoirs* really Memoirs in the sense in which this
word is so over-used, so profaned? Is this biography of M. de
Chateaubriand really a biography? No. The *Memoirs* of M. de
Chateaubriand are simply a vast poem in which are amassed helter-

skelter all the loves, all the hatreds, all the passions, all the pretentions, all the greatness, all the defeats of this century. The Republic, the Empire, the Church, the Monarch, the Constitution, the fears and the hopes, the past and the future of modern France, that is what this book is. (I, 40)

A scientific history attempts, or should attempt, to be as all-inclusive as possible within the limits of purpose set by the author. Not so with Chateaubriand. There is a very careful choice of material to be presented. One of the prime considerations in this choice is the question of tone.

In a very general and consistent way, Chateaubriand sought to exclude from the *Memoirs* all that was common or base, whether it concerned himself or others. There is a kind of Olympian tone and stature to the work, a transposition of all that is low and ordinary into something lofty and extraordinary. Chateaubriand, as a true Romantic, prefers to survey the landscape from the mountaintop, literally and figuratively. The observations of the ant are out of place.

This leads him into silence or distortion concerning many of the incidents in his life. As we have already seen, Chateaubriand excluded from the *Memoirs* all mention of his career as a stocking salesman. He explains his absence from Paris to attend to this business by inventing an illness which supposedly kept him in bed. In the same way, when George Washington was too ill to receive Chateaubriand, the idea was unthinkable for the author, so he invented the protracted interview with the American president.

Other, less personal examples of the technique are to be found at every step. Certain spiteful remarks and descriptions centering on Napoleon disappear from the early manuscripts of the *Memoirs*: in spite of Chateaubriand's intense dislike for the emperor, he realized such pettiness was out of place and would add a jarring note. In the same way, some bitter and repeated remarks concerning the ingratitude of the Bourbons disappeared, partly at the insistence of Mme de Chateaubriand and others, but also as a part of this elevated and detached attitude which so characterizes the *Memoirs*.

This type of modification can easily be documented: the many manuscripts, the letters, and the reports of Chateaubriand's confidants all tend to show this was a conscious and deliberate process. The result is most felicitous. The value of memoirs is, again, not as history, because they are by the very nature of the genre partial and distorted. Their true value lies in the interpretation of the individual and the society as seen through the eyes of an acute observer and a writer of genius. Without this transfiguration of persons and events, the *Memoirs* would remain on the level of countless other collections of authentic and apocryphal memoirs which abounded at the time.

The last of these general considerations is perhaps the most important: narrative technique. It is pointless to attempt to determine to what extent Chateaubriand's particular technique is the result of a conscious effort and to what extent it is subconscious. Certainly, had Chateaubriand died at the age of sixty, the physical circumstances would have prevented the full development of the narrative technique we shall describe. On the other hand, there is much evidence that the workings of Chateaubriand's mind dictated this specific kind of technique which he consciously strove to achieve. However, planned or fortuitous, this highly sophisticated technique exists, a technique at times startlingly modern in its innovations, capable of impressing the reader of today as few works of the nineteenth century can.

Although on the surface of the *Memoirs* we find a straightforward recital of the events in chronological order, a closer examination shows an extreme complexity of construction. First and foremost, Chateaubriand carries us along with a double narrative, each following its own timetable. The events of his life form one chronology, but the events surrounding the dates of composition of the various books of the *Memoirs* have their own separate order. Thus, the Chateaubriand who is minister to the Prussian court of 1821 coexists with the youth of prerevolutionary days. The ambassador in England coexists with the penniless émigré of 1793. Generally, at the beginning of each book, or sometimes at the beginning of a section of a book, he takes pains to stop and remind us that the man who is describing the events is not the one who was experiencing them.

The effect is heightened by auxiliary techniques. We have seen how many years were spanned by the writing and the revising of the *Memoirs*. Frequently the revisions made over the years are simply inserted in the text. More often, however, the additions are put in footnotes which are dated, giving the reader a double perspective on the events described. Thus the event of 1790 is described in 1821, but this description is modified, the focus changed, the emphasis shifted, the color attenuated or defined, in an addition of 1831.

There is, finally, an extreme fluidity of time in the narrative gained through a constant use of anticipation and flashback. Chateaubriand hints at what he will say later in the work, or he returns to dwell on events which predate the period he happens to be dealing with.

The technique we have described would have been considered revolutionary in a novel of the time. The unstructured form of memoirs, however, was more open to such innovation, and indeed these innovations probably went largely unnoticed by nineteenth-century readers. Yet it is certain that a great deal of the attraction of the *Memoirs* for the reader of today resides precisely in this technique, which so closely approximates certain aspects of the modern novel.

As the book progresses, the double lines of chronology start to converge, since the pace of narration is more rapid than the pace of the events. The times he is describing come closer and closer to the time of composition, so that the time lag narrows. As the events come closer, the action takes on an interest and a rapidity which seem to recall the action of a classical tragedy rushing to its inevitable end. This is of course literary illusion, not actuality. As a matter of fact, the earlier portions are perforce described more rapidly, and the earlier scenes show in reality a Chateaubriand who is much more active than the older Chateaubriand of the end of the *Memoirs*. This extraordinary time sequence creates a magnificent ending for a work which so easily could have relaxed into platitude. Instead of becoming bored with an old man growing weaker, more arthritic, less active day by day, we are breathlessly living each moment of his life with Chateaubriand. When his active life finishes, the *Memoirs* are at an end.

Once these general considerations are put aside, however, the work can be seen to derive much of its force from three particular elements: portraits, associations, and contrasts.

V *Portraits*

Chateaubriand excels in portraits. His *Memoirs* are studded with them throughout. It is not without reason that Molière has his pseudo-intellectual say in *Les Précieuses ridicules*: "Portraits are difficult, and require a deep mind." Those who indulge in difficult literary forms without the requisite wit, as is the case with the characters in the play, succeed only in making themselves ridiculous. Chateaubriand, on the other hand, has the ability, in a short space, to sum up all the important traits of a personality. These portraits are of three general types: political figures, literary figures, and close friends.

Portraits of Napoleon abound. The most famous is perhaps to be found in the parallel portraits of Washington and Bonaparte. However, Napoleon's shadow so looms over the nineteenth century that he reappears constantly in the *Memoirs*. Each aspect of his character is analyzed with skill. In this passage, for example, we have the portrait of Napoleon the statesman:

. . . Bonaparte was a poet in action, an immense genius in war, an untiring mind, skilful and sensible in administration, a laborious and responsible legislator. That is why he has such a hold on the imagination of peoples, and so much authority over the judgment of positive men. But as a man of politics, he will always be one who is defective in the eyes of the statesmen. This observation, which has escaped most of his panegyrists, will become, I am convinced, the definitive opinion which will remain of him; it will explain the contrast between his prodigious actions and their miserable results. At Saint Helena he himself severely condemned his political conduct on two points: the Spanish campaign and the Russian campaign; he could have extended his confession to other sins. Perhaps his enthusiasts will not maintain that in these admissions he was mistaken about himself. Let us recapitulate:

Bonaparte acted against all prudence, without mentioning again the odious aspect of the action, in killing the Duke d'Enghien: he hung a weight around his own neck. In spite of the childish apologists, this death, as we have seen, was the secret leavening of the discord which later broke out between [Czar] Alexander and Napoleon, as between Prussia and France.

The Spanish undertaking was completely abusive: the Peninsula belonged to the Emperor; he could have gained any advantage: instead of that he made of it a training school for the English soldiers, and created the principle of his own destruction, that of the popular uprising.

The detention of the Pope, and the annexing of the Church States to France was only the caprice of tyranny through which he lost his advantage of passing for the restorer of religion.

Bonaparte did not stop when he had married the daughter of the Caesars, as he should have done: Russia and England were crying for mercy.

He did not resuscitate Poland, when the salvation of Europe depended on the reestablishment of that kingdom.

He threw himself at Russia, in spite of the warnings of his generals and advisors.

Once the folly had begun, he advanced beyond Smolensk; everything told him that he should go no further in his first move, that his first campaign in the North was finished, and that the second (he felt it himself) would make him master of the empire of the Czars.

He was incapable of computing the number of days or of foreseeing the effect of the climate, while everyone in Moscow computed and foresaw. See in its proper place what I have had to say about the *continental blockade* and the *Rhine Confederation;* the first, a gigantic conception but a doubtful accomplishment; the second, a considerable undertaking, but vitiated in its execution by campaign instinct and the fiscal mentality. Napoleon received as a gift the old French monarchy, created by the centuries and an uninterrupted succession of great men, just as it had been left by the majesty of Louis XIV and the alliances of Louis XV, just as it had been enlarged by the Republic. He sat down on this magnificent pedestal, stretched out his arms, caught hold of entire peoples, and drew them to him; but he lost Europe as promptly as he had taken it; twice he brought the allies to Paris, in spite of the miracles of his military intelligence. He had the world at his feet and he drew from it only a prison for himself, exile for his family, the loss of all his conquests and even the loss of a part of the old French soil. (Book 24, Chapter 5)

Next to the political portraits must be placed the literary portraits. Chateaubriand knew all the figures active in the world of letters in his time, and he knew how to interpret them with incisive candor.

One of the earliest literary portraits belongs to Chateaubriand's first years in Paris in the 1780's. This portion of the *Memoirs* was composed in 1821. As an aspiring author, Chateaubriand was anxious to meet all of the reigning literary greats. One of these was the poet Evariste Parny. Today Parny is completely forgotten, but in his day he influenced generations of authors throughout Europe and delighted his multitude of readers. Chateaubriand arranged a visit to the famous poet:

I knew by heart the elegies of the Chevalier de Parny, and I still know them. I wrote to him to ask permission to see a poet whose works were a delight to me: he answered politely: I went to see him on the rue de Cléry.

I found a man still fairly young, very refined, tall, thin, his face marked from smallpox. He returned my visit; I presented him to my sisters. He cared little for society, and he was soon driven from it by politics: he was then of the old party. I have known no other author who was more like his works: a poet and a creole, he needed only the sky of India, a fountain, a palm tree, and a woman. He feared noise, sought to slip through life without being seen, sacrificed everything to his indolence, and was betrayed in his obscurity only by his pleasures which in passing touched his lyre:

> I would that life, in happiness and joy,
> Might flow unseen, and sheltered by Love's wing,
> A rivulet, content to murmur low,
> Within its bed containing all its waves,
> And seeking out the shade of thick-set shrubs:
> It would not dare to venture through the plain. (4, 12)[5]

In the span of a few brief words Chateaubriand has managed to characterize the man both physically and on the literary level. This is the basic purpose of the portrait, so suited to the talent of Chateaubriand and so successfully utilized throughout the *Memoirs*.

Jean-François de La Harpe was another writer of only secondary importance today, but who played a great role as poet and critic. When Chateaubriand, in the course of his chronological narration, reaches the date of La Harpe's death, 1803, he presents his portrait of the man. It is perhaps worth noting that this portrait had already been announced much earlier in the *Memoirs* (4, 12) in the same episode of the early trip to Paris in which Chateaubriand met Parny. Chateaubriand frequently makes use of this kind of physical bond among various parts of the work which he creates by this kind of cross-reference.

This is how Chateaubriand sees La Harpe:

I arrived [in Paris] in time to see the death of a man who belonged to those superior beings of the second rank, in the eighteenth century, who form a solid background to society, giving that society breadth and conscience.

I had met M. de La Harpe in 1789: as Flins had done, he was taken by a fine infatuation for my sister, the countess de Farcy. He arrived with three weighty tomes of his works in his little arms, quite astonished that his glory did not triumph over the most rebellious hearts. With a high-pitched voice and an expressive face, he would inveigh against abuses, ordering an omelette at the table of ministers of state when he found the dinner of poor quality, eating with his fingers, dragging his sleeves in the dishes, serving up philosophical crudities to the greatest nobles, who delighted in his insolence; but withal, an upright spirit, enlightened, impartial in the midst of his passions, capable of recognizing talent and admiring it, capable of weeping over a beautiful line of poetry or a beautiful action, and having a depth of character capable of bearing repentance. He was true to his destiny: I saw him die as a courageous Christian, his taste broadened by religion, keeping only his scorn of impiety and his hatred of *revolutionary language*. (14, 4)

Chateaubriand did not limit his portraits to the secondary authors. Some of his most interesting remarks deal with George Sand. However, the evaluation is perhaps more revealing of the attitudes of Chateaubriand's generation than of the literary value of George Sand:

Madame Sand possesses a talent of the first order; her descriptions have the reality of those of Rousseau in his *Rêveries*, and of Bernardin de Saint-Pierre in his *Studies*. Her frank style is blotted by none of the faults of the day. *Lélia*, painful to read, and which does not offer some of the delightful scenes of *Indiana* and *Valentine*, is nevertheless a masterpiece in its genre: in the nature of an orgy, it is without passion, and it troubles like a passion; the soul is absent from it, and yet it makes the heart heavy; the depraving of the maxims of life, the insult to decency, could not possibly go further; but into this abyss the author lowers her talent. In the valley of Gomorrha, dew falls at night on the Dead Sea. . . .

These novels, poetry in their subject matter, are born out of the times. In spite of her superiority, it is to be feared that Madame Sand has, by the very nature of her writings, narrowed the circle of her readers. George Sand will never belong to all times. If there are two men of equal genius, one preaching order and the other disorder, the first will attract the larger number of listeners: human kind refuses unanimous approval of what attacks morality, the pillow on which sleep the meek and the just. . . .

I have not seen Madame Sand dressed as a man or wearing a shirt and carrying the iron-pointed staff of the mountain climber: I have not seen her drink from the cup of the bacchantes and smoke indolently seated on a sofa like a sultana: natural or affected eccentricities which for me add nothing to her charm or her genius. (43, 8)

Perhaps the most moving of Chateaubriand's portraits are the personal ones. When he has a great deal of affection for an individual, this affection makes itself felt. Mme Récamier, on the personal level, occupies perhaps the same rank as Napoleon on the political. Her role in the writing of the *Memoirs* was exceedingly important, just as she had been one of the great guiding influences in all of Chateaubriand's life, so that we find frequent reference to her in the work. Sometimes it is a rapid paragraph, giving only a brief glimpse of the subject:

I have followed in her footsteps, this traveler, on the path that she has scarcely trodden; soon I shall precede her in another land. As she wanders in the midst of these *Memoirs,* in the secret corners of this basilica I am hastening to complete, she may come across this chapel which I dedicate to her here; perhaps she will be pleased to rest there a while: I have put her image there. (29, 23)

In these words, presumably written almost ten years before his death, it is revealing to find meditation on that subject so prominent in Chateaubriand's mind. Book 29 of the *Memoirs* in its entirety, is a long portrait and history of Mme Récamier. It is one of the most successful pieces of the entire work.

Chateaubriand's affection for his elder sister Lucile quite understandably was another highly personal influence at work in the *Memoirs.* The portrait of her declining days, both her health and her mind near collapse, is particularly touching:

She was penniless: I had chosen an apartment for her on the rue Caumartin, deceiving her about the price of the rent and the arrangements I had her make with a restaurateur. Like a flame about to go out, her genius glowed with the most brilliant light; she was quite illuminated by it. She would scribble a few lines which she would then throw into the fire, or else she would copy out of books thoughts which were in harmony with her state of mind. (17, 6)

After receiving news of Lucile's death, he muses on the sadness of her end:

I have prepared many tombs in my life; it was my fate and that of my sister that her ashes were scattered to the winds. I was not in Paris at the moment of her death; I had not a single relative there; kept at Villeneuve by the perilous state of my wife's health, I could not rush to stand by the sacred remains; orders transmitted from afar arrived too late to avoid a common burial. Lucile was alone and friendless; she was known only to the old servant of Mme de Beaumont, as if he had been fated to bind together their two destinies. He alone followed the abandoned casket, and he died himself before Mme de Chateaubriand had sufficiently recovered for me to take her back to Paris.

My sister was buried among the poor: in what cemetery was she laid to rest? In what motionless wave of the ocean of the dead was she swallowed up? (17, 6)

VI *Role of Associations*

As in all of Chateaubriand, the role of associations is paramount. Chateaubriand was always living not only in the present but simultaneously in the past. It will be remembered that Chateaubriand, disgusted with government service, was unwilling to accept any post, until the ambassadorship to Rome was offered him. The historic associations of the Eternal City were so strong as to overcome any reluctance he may have had. Everything in Rome suggests the past: the monuments, the ruins, the churches, the papacy itself.

If the associations are inappropriate, Chateaubriand immediately senses this. For example, when he traveled in Protestant countries and visited the churches which were originally Catholic, he sensed a conflict between the present purpose and the past associations of the buildings. On the other hand, when the associations are in tune with the present, the effect is one of reinforcing every sight, every action with the weight of centuries of history.

Thus, while he was in Rome, dealing with the pope and politics, he immediately recalled the recent history of Napoleon's abduction of Pope Pius VII in 1809. The associations did not stop here, however. Immediately the mind of Chateaubriand was flooded with memories of the similar situation of Boniface VIII and Philippe le Bel in 1303 (39, 9).

Proust did not hesitate to indicate his debt to Chateaubriand in this area of unconscious memory. Just as in Proust's case, the overwhelming effect of these associations is produced by their being automatic. The effect is lost if one has to search out the associations. With Chateaubriand, it is enough to enter a church to be overcome with emotions suggested by the subconscious associations whose overwhelming force is immediately felt, but which can be brought to the surface consciousness only by a process of examination and analysis.

In all of his writings, one of Chateaubriand's favorite techniques is juxtaposition of disparate elements which form a kind of counterpoint when taken together. Sometimes the contrast is one of tone, sometimes it is a contrast of point of view or content. This technique is one of the most frequently recurring elements in the *Memoirs*. To this end, Chateaubriand included a great deal of his diplomatic correspondence in the *Memoirs*. Certainly this is to be explained partly by the author's desire to show his importance as a diplomat, and he even goes so far as to justify these inclusions by saying "my diplomatic correspondence is, I believe, on a par with my literary compositions" (34, 10), but this is true in a certain sense. No one reads this correspondence for its intrinsic value. But taken as one of those elements designed to add another dimension, another facet, to the picture being painted, it serves an important and admirable function.

In this way, in the description of the Roman ambassadorship, Chateaubriand carries on a three-level narrative composed of the day-to-day journal of events which presumably was composed on the spot at the time, set off on one hand by the personal letters to Mme Récamier and on the other hand the official dispatches sent back to the foreign office. All of this is held together by the analytical hindsight of the later narration. Each one of the facets has an existence of its own which would have been destroyed had all three elements simply been combined. However, if they are merely juxtaposed, as Chateaubriand presents them, a startling effect of simultaneity is created.

A similarly effective use of contrast of disparate materials occurs in the portion of the *Memoirs* dealing with the duchess de Berry (36, 1). The cholera epidemic then sweeping France offered the duchess an opportunity to indulge in some ostentatious and politically oriented charity. She entrusted Chateaubriand with some funds to be offered to the stricken. The civic officials were most wary about accepting any money, feeling the danger of the politics outweighed the advantages of the money to the cholera victims. The archbishop of Paris, however, accepted the money with good grace. Chateaubriand reproduces in his *Memoirs* the letters he received from one of the antilegitimist city officials refusing the money, and the letter from the archbishop accepting it. The simple juxtaposition of the two letters, one petty and suspicious, the other lofty and noble, immediately serves Chateaubriand's purpose of discrediting the city officials in the eyes of his readers, and exalting the churchman (and at the same time justifying the cause of the duchess).

A third, slightly different application of the technique is to be found in that portion of the text describing the trip to the Near East. Chateaubriand's servant, Julien, kept a diary during the trip. The counterpoint of passages from Julien's diary against Chateaubriand's own narrative again serves to give depth to what could otherwise have remained two-dimensional.

It is significant that this is a conscious process directed toward gaining a multiple point of view. The material, which can at times appear as extraneous "filler," is never that. Chateaubriand uses his "documentation" with care and with purpose. When his purpose would not be served by the inclusion of such material, it was not used. One immediately thinks of the example of Mme de Chateaubriand's memoirs. Chateaubriand had asked her to compose these, but his interest was only in having something to refresh his memory about dates and events. He did not intend Mme de Chateaubriand to have any significant role to play in the literary work. Thus, Céleste's memoirs are not used in the contrapuntal way the other documents we have seen were used.

These examples are only a few of those figuring in this constantly recurring technique of the *Memoirs*. The result of this constant introduction of outside material, which after all is traditional in the genre of memoirs, could well have involved nothing new or noteworthy in the hands of an ordinary writer. Once more, however, Chateaubriand with his usual ability to turn everything to gold, gave purpose and value to the technique, exploiting it to produce previously unrealized multiple layers of meaning.

VII *Duality of the Work in Tone and Subject*

This double point of view, the double aspect, lofty and base at the same time, recalls the duality of much of Spanish Literature. Chateaubriand and Julien, for example, are the Don Quixote and Sancho Panza of another age. Indeed, the quixotic side of Chateaubriand's nature has often been the subject of critics. Just as the Spanish novel would have been imperfect without the proper blend of high and low, Chateaubriand's work requires a similar admixture. The Olympian tone after which he strove so valiantly requires some kind of relief.

There is also a comparison to be made here with *René*. No doubt, Chateaubriand chose to paint one side of his own character, the romantic and melancholy reveries, in *René*. At the same time, he was clear-headed enough to evaluate these reveries for what they were, in himself and in his character René. That is why the old missionary appears at the end of *René* to deliver some cold and reasonable sermons to the young man. In the same way, Chateaubriand, with all his pretensions and aspirations, sees the need to bring his account down to earth from time to time by reproducing some of Julien's sanchoesque practicalities. Chateaubriand must often have thought of one particular fable of La Fontaine, one of his favorite authors. In "The Milkmaid and the Milk Jug," the milkmaid, lost in her daydreams, is brought back to earth when she lets slip the jug and spills the milk she is carrying to market, thus ending the elaborate daydreams of what she would do with the money. La Fontaine ends by moralizing:

> What mind doesn't run wild?
> Who doesn't build castles in the air? . . .
> Everyone dreams while he is awake . . .
> Everything in the world belongs to us . . .
> When some accident bring me back to myself,
> I'm just plain old John, as before. (VI, 10)

Chateaubriand, too, lets his mind wander in fantasy, but he is always ready, at the appropriate moment, to inject some "accident" which returns him to himself.

How can one sum up the *Memoirs*? It is an impossible task. The *Memoirs* are an entire universe which by its very nature escapes any attempt at codification. It is easy to say that the work does not present an accurate portrait either of the author or of his times. But what is an accurate portrait? The coldly calculated analysis of a historian may well give an accurate portrait, but it does not correspond to anything experienced by those living at the times and who of necessity had a very personal and biased view of the times.

Chateaubriand sometimes dwells on this very question of truth and impartiality:

Will the work inspired by my ashes and destined for my ashes live on after me? Perhaps my work is without value; perhaps when they see the light of day these *Memoirs* will fade away. At least the things that I shall have described for myself will have served to allay the boredom of those last hours no one wants and with which one knows not what to do. At the end of life there lies a bitter age: nothing is agreeable, because one is worthless; good for no one, a burden on everyone, near to the last resting place, there is only one step to be taken to reach it: what use is there in dreaming on a deserted strand? What pleasant shades would be visible in the future? Fie on the clouds now circling my head!

An idea keeps coming back to me and troubling me: my conscience is not reassured of the innocence of my hours of work; I blame my blindness and the obliging nature of man towards his faults. Is what I have written really just? Are ethics and charity strictly observed? Of what use would repentance be if these *Memoirs* were to do some harm? (44, 8)

There is a higher truth to which Chateaubriand is faithful, just as Balzac was to be faithful. Balzac is no more the accurate historian of his times than Chateaubriand, yet both authors were able to seize the essence of an epoch as they saw it and as they interpreted it, infusing the portrait with a transcendent reality surpassing any ordinary representation.

Chateaubriand's grave is on a tiny island off the shore of Saint-Malo. According to his instructions, the tomb is perfectly plain, only the date and a cross. Jean-Paul Sartre found this to be false simplicity and in truth only monumental presumption, and he proceeded, according to Simone de Beauvoir, to indicate his scorn in an unmistakable fashion. But Chateaubriand was right: he had no need of an elaborate inscription detailing his works and achievements; the *Memoirs from Beyond the Grave* do indeed serve their purpose as his monument after death. The ancient Egyptians multiplied the inscriptions bearing the cartouches of their reigning pharaohs in the belief that as long as the name was visible the man would continue to be known and he would thus gain immortality. But, in truth, the pharaohs gained their immortality through their works, and such is the case with Chateaubriand. As usual, it is Chateaubriand himself who states the idea with the greatest of clarity and the maximum of effectiveness:

Meanwhile, busying myself with the idea of writing my *Memoirs,* I appreciated the price the ancients attached to the value of their names: there is perhaps a touching reality in this perpetuating of the memories one can leave as he passes by. Perhaps, among the great men of antiquity, that idea of immortality for the human race took the place of our concept of the immortality of the soul, which remained problematical for them. If fame is of little import when it concerns only us, we must still admit that it is a fine privilege attached to the friendship of genius which makes it possible to give imperishable existence to all it has loved. (15, 7)

CHAPTER 10

Style

I *Difficulty of Analysis*

STYLE is an exceedingly difficult topic to treat when dealing with a native author. When the question of style must be dealt with in relation to a foreign writer, the problem becomes almost insoluble. The question of translation falsifies any remarks one can make on the subject, and the differences in stylistic tradition in the histories of French and English literature have produced a veritable gulf separating them.

If one is to deal adequately with Chateaubriand, however, the question of style cannot be neglected. It is so fundamental a part of his work, and his importance as a writer is so bound up with the element of style, that an effort must be made to gain at least a certain amount of insight into the topic.

Style can most easily be opposed to content: content is what the author says; style is how he says it. The effectiveness with which an idea or a scene is presented depends on the qualities of style and the writer's skill in using them.

There has been a long tradition of perfection in style in French literature. Those authors such as La Fontaine and Flaubert who excelled in the art of expression made it one of the essential elements of their writings. Inspired by their example, writers whose styles were less acceptable in the polished classical scene, such as Balzac, deemed it necessary to spend endless hours on their manuscripts, attempting to give them the stylistic brilliance which they found lacking.

It was this long tradition of style as an essential component of literary achievement which allowed the mid-twentieth-century development in France of the "new novel" where style takes such prominence that the matter of the novel all but ceases to exist. It is no surprise that the "new novelists" traced their techniques back to Flaubert, where the beginnings of a preponderance of form over matter is distinctly visible.

151

In Chateaubriand, however, form serves matter. In every case, Chateaubriand's stylistic genius is not turned in upon itself but rather serves to paint a visual or mental picture: the beauties of a primitive sunset, the anxieties of an emotion.

II *Classicism and Romanticism: Constraint and Freedom*

As is true of Chateaubriand's work in general, the style is a combination of Classicism and Romanticism. His formal education was a classical one. The passages of the *Memoirs* in which he talks of his favorite books, his favorite quotations, involve almost always the Latin and Greek classics, the French Classical authors of the seventeenth century, and occasionally the classics of other European literatures. *The Lusiads* of Camõens seems to have been a particular favorite, for example, and the translation of Milton's *Paradise Lost* was merely a culmination of Chateaubriand's long appreciation of the English classics.

Part of Chateaubriand's school work consisted of stylistic exercises involving imitations of these classical writers. A thorough knowledge of all the figures of rhetoric and their use formed an essential element of this education. Thus, in his mature writings, we find Chateaubriand using those same carefully architectured, balanced phrases and figures that recall the ancients and their modern disciples. At times, the English-speaking reader may look for these elements in vain. Modern English simply does not lend itself to the long, ornate developments that are possible in French. The usual practice among translators is to break up a single sentence into two or three when putting it into English. Otherwise, the result can be enormously cumbersome, and what is beautiful in French becomes awkward in English.

Chateaubriand's tendency in French is to lean toward very long sentences which for the most part involve parallel developments. At times, he carries on two separate ideas in relation to one another; at times, he develops contrary aspects of one idea; at times, he contrasts one individual with another.

The actual language used in these sentences is worthy of special attention. It is frequently described as "poetic"; and indeed, the prose of Chateaubriand is very close to poetry. Yet at the same time, Chateaubriand was never very much at home in true poetry. This is a fact often remarked not only by the critics but by Chateaubriand himself. The explanation of this paradox—a most poetic author who does not write poetry but prose—lies in the combination of Classical and Romantic elements in the author's style.

For the author's frequent apostrophes to liberty involve not only political and personal liberty but also literary liberty. Perhaps Chateaubriand was not himself entirely aware of the extent to which he required freedom in his writing, but the evidence is present almost everywhere to support this statement. Perhaps *The Natchez* offers one of the best examples. As we have seen, Chateaubriand devoutly desired to write an epic poem. From the beginning, he abandoned the idea of verse, but he began by attempting to give to the work all the other exterior trappings of the traditional epic. Halfway through he gave up the attempt and reverted to straightforward narrative. The work remains nonetheless an epic, and perhaps one of the most successful of modern epics.

The "elbow room" Chateaubriand found necessary within the genre of the epic he finds necessary everywhere. While remaining true to the basic requirements of poetry, he finds it necessary to reject the too-constraining elements of form.

It is important to realize that the verse poets contemporary with Chateaubriand were for the most part far less adventuresome. They did indeed change the matter, giving it an entirely new orientation toward the Romantic insistence on sensitivity and individualism over logic and generalization,, but they remained largely prisoners of the old forms. The other experiments with the prose poem, and with irregular verse forms, had to await the middle of the nineteenth century and were not fully realized until the twentieth century.

Again, Chateaubriand may not have fully realized his innovation, and contemporary critics most certainly did not. They spent long pages of their articles trying to explain why Chateaubriand did not write in verse, with sometimes ludicrous "explanations."

Chateaubriand's subject matter was therefore too large to fit into the old mold. The new mold fashioned by Chateaubriand was not a real mold at all but a kind of formless and pliable sack which would take on the shape of whatever form was put into it. The important and essential element of this non-form was a poetic aura existing outside the general concept of poetry. This aura was created by means of two techniques: the insertion of poetic elements into prose, and the massive use of imagery, which of course in the broader sense is just another of the poetic elements referred to in the first of the techniques. We have taken "poetic elements" to mean here, however, the most basic elements of language.

III *French Prosody*

French poetry, unlike English, is not based on a recurring pattern of stress accents. It has what is known as a mathematical base; that is, it utilizes a recurring pattern in the number of syllables. The effectiveness of this in the creation of poetic prose can be readily seen. In English, a line of iambic pentameter, for example, occurring in the midst of a prose passage, would be obvious and annoying. It would not at all produce the effect created where a phrase of six syllables or twelve syllables occurred in a French prose text. The foundation of poetry in French is much more subtle, so that its effects, especially in prose, are likewise much more subtle. The reader can come across a line of verse in French prose and be unaware of it on a conscious level, so that he is left merely with a poetic impression whose source he does not recognize unless he analyzes the passage.

The most common pattern in French poetry is a line composed of two six-syllable segments. The line must divide itself naturally and logically into these segments. An examination of almost any of Chateaubriand's French texts will indicate that there are countless six-syllable segments scattered throughout the prose, and occasional twelve-syllable segments. Also, at times, there will be seen to appear patterns of two six-syllable segments separated by other developments.

The whole process is, of course, infinitely more complicated, going into the niceties of the less common verse forms and making use of much more involved techniques, but this analysis can serve to describe the basic technique used by Chateaubriand.

In addition, alliteration is used extensively. This too is less immediately recognizable since its use as a poetic technique had been far more restricted in French poetry up to that time than in English, so that what would appear a moderate use of alliteration to English ears would be impressive to the French ear.

IV *Imagery, Color, and Description*

On this foundation of poetic form is built the edifice of poetic expression largely through the use of images and color. Here again there is a combination of Classicism and Romanticism, of tradition and freedom. Chateaubriand is very much inclined to the classical image, even when his description covers a subject far from those traditions. For example, Chateaubriand sees no contradiction in describing the moon as Diana's chariot, even though the subject is the wilds of America. But this is a part of Chateaubriand's technique: he is continually explaining the unknown in the terms of the known. When he is describing a far away place, his comparison is drawn from the experience, actual or literary, of his readers. Thus, since few Frenchmen had seen a papaya tree, Chateaubriand described the fruit hanging on the tree as reminding him of the crystals hanging down from candlesticks.

In this same way, the images usually do double service: they explain the phenomenon and add to the color and richness of the description. It is because of the appropriateness and the usefulness of these images that they serve the author so well. An obvious embellishment which existed only for itself would not produce the same artistic effect as the same element performing a function. To take Gothic architecture as an example, a comparison that would certainly be to Chateaubriand's taste, the excesses of the nineteenth-century imitation Gothic came from the fact that the architecture and the embellishments no longer were functional. The outward forms were preserved in the mistaken idea that they alone were important. There is always, however, an unseen force acting upon the esthetic effect —the function.

This is the way in which Chateaubriand manages to use an incredible number of images without making them seem excessive. "Everything must be put in its proper place," said Chateaubriand in *The Genius of Christianity*, and he put this idea into practice with his images: they serve a definite and multiple purpose wherever they appear.

Next to the basic Classicism of this technique there is the same abandon, the same liberty that can be found in the more literal of the poetic elements. The nature of the images is such that they evoke an exotic visual effect, frequently involving an incredible profusion of color and movement. Historians of art point to the differences between the Classic painter David and the Romantic painter Delacroix by emphasizing the static nature of the former, his sublime repose and tranquillity, while the Romantic painter fills his canvas with color and motion. Much the same could be said of Chateaubriand contrasted with the Classical authors.

This comparison with art is most appropriate. The one over-whelming impression that comes from Chateaubriand's descriptions is a visual one. Other elements, such as sound and odor, are not absent, but they are auxiliary in their function. Above all, Chateaubriand seeks to create a vision. Chateaubriand may well be without equal in French literature in this descriptive power. Perhaps Zola is the only author capable of such intense literary depiction; however, his totally different technique and subject matter make a comparison fruitless. Chateaubriand in his own particular domain—the vivid and tumultuous reproduction of visual tableaux—reigns supreme.

V   *Overall Evaluation*

Frequently in the course of examining Chateaubriand's individual works it has been necessary to recognize that certain of them taken as a whole have only historic interest to the reader of today, except for a few "anthology pages" which have survived. For the ordinary writer this would be tantamount to condemnation. But in these cases Chateaubriand cannot be properly judged except as a poet.

With the traditional poets of the past it is rare indeed that all segments of the complete work have maintained equal interest. A handful of poems out of an entire collection are ample reason to give the poet an enviable reputation. So with Chateaubriand, these few pages out of a much larger work represent poems in prose, complete in themselves and entirely capable of an existence apart from the work of which, physically, they form a segment.

Once more, it is because of this poetic nature of much of Chateaubriand's text that the question of style assumes such overwhelming importance. He so carefully combines the elements of sound, balance, and image, that his writings take on a life and an intensity to be found nowhere else.

In the field of stylistics, Chateaubriand is never less than a master craftsman. At his least good he represents the culmination of all the traditions of eighteenth-century rhetoric and style. But at his best, as seen to such advantage in the *Life of Rancé,* he is not only the master craftsman but a genuine innovator whose stylistic experiments allow him to do things never before attempted; and in this, Chateaubriand is eminently successful. When a nineteenth-century author can still startle the public and the critics of the twentieth century by the newness of his style, there can be no question of his success.

CHAPTER 11

Conclusion

NO one disputes today the important place of Chateaubriand as a world author. The number of English translations, as can be seen in the Bibliography, is ample proof in itself. The English translations can be matched by others in all the world's languages.

The only discussions concern the exact nature of his influence and importance. For example, Chateaubriand has for so long been the idol of an elite, so long been the object of an admiration to no small extent tinged with snobism, that many consider him an author not for the masses. True, Chateaubriand is no Alexander Dumas. And yet he may not be so divorced from the general public as one might be led to believe. One recent critic accused Chateaubriand's work of having about it "something haughty and distant which deprives it of homely warmth and forceful simplicity, qualities equally accessible to the refined and the humble."

There is a certain truth to this. In France today, Chateaubriand is not read to the extent that Zola, Balzac, and Dumas are. Nonetheless, he remains an author who is widely read, studied, and admired.

What measures of an author's importance may we use? First, the activity of the critics. A glance at any current bibliography will show the enormous amount of scholarly interest being inspired today by Chateaubriand. What have these critics done? They have analyzed the work, exploring its beauties, and they have traced the beginnings of many modern literary schools and developments back to Chateaubriand. In the same way, authors such as Proust, early in the century, and Gracq, Butor, and Jouhandeau today, have indicated their debt to and admiration for Chateaubriand. The modern literary scene would not today be precisely what it is but for him.

Students of all countries read Chateaubriand. He is an integral part of any program of nineteenth-century French literature.

However, it is true that students sometimes read not what they want, but what is forced upon them, so that this as a criterion for lasting greatness is perhaps not too convincing a one.

The criterion which is convincing is the reaction of the current general reading public. In France, at the present moment, for example, the prospective purchaser has the choice of five complete editions of the *Memoirs from Beyond the Grave*: one for every taste, every purpose, every pocketbook. One edition is beautifully bound and illustrated and sells to the collector for a high price. Another edition is full of notes and designed for the serious student and the scholar. Another is a well-bound library edition. But it is perhaps the two other editions currently in print which are particularly important. One is the *Livre de Poche*, literally "pocket book," in the popular format of detective stories and other paperbacks destined for mass consumption. The fact that this edition in three volumes of seven hundred pages each, formidable by its size alone, and written by a nineteenth-century author, can successfully compete with popular twentieth-century novels, is convincing testimony as to the work's readership of today. Another edition belongs to a series delivered with a kind of book-of-the-month plan. Chateaubriand shares billing with Dumas, Hugo, Stendhal, George Sand, and a host of other popular authors. Even more convincing proof of Chateaubriand's power: the prospective reader has a free choice among the offered books, taking only what interests him. Even under such circumstances Chateaubriand can hold his own.

There is, therefore, undeniably an enormous readership of Chateaubriand in France today. At present there are almost forty separate editions of various works of Chateaubriand available to the public. The phenomenon is obviously not limited to the *Memoirs* by any means. Outside France, readership has been gained less rapidly, mainly through the lack of currently available translations, but that lack is rapidly being remedied.

What do all these readers find in Chateaubriand today? First, in today's literary environment, which frequently prizes form above content, they find one of the most perfect forms of expression known in literature. The force of a passage from Chateaubriand, existing only for itself, is a phenomenon which cannot perhaps be satisfactorily explained but which is nonetheless clearly observable. The reason for the immediacy of response to these texts on the part of the modern reader has been docu-

mented in the preceding chapters. Time and again it is obvious
that Chateaubriand's processes, even though fitted to the Romantic and even Classical mold, go far beyond those earlier concepts
in the realm of structure and imagery. Chateaubriand's skill at
joining together unlikely combinations is perhaps at the basis
of his continued ability to affect the reader. Nothing is easier
than to construct an image or a comparison made up of seemingly irreconcilable elements. But to be successful, the irrecon-
cilables must somehow be reconciled. This is the role of genius.
The great danger of such an attempt is that the result may
be merely ridiculous rather than being a marvelous accomplishment, striking in its dazzling newness. This technique requires
the unerring taste of a Chateaubriand in order that such materials
may be dealt with effectively. Just as there is only a hairline
between the designer of taste who can put together the colors
which set each other off, on the one hand, and the tasteless
imitator who assembles colors which clash in visual cacophony,
on the other, only that indefinable standard of taste can separate
the great literary artist from the artless imitator. Time and again
we have seen evidence of Chateaubriand's ability to stop always
at precisely the right point, never overstepping the bounds
of taste.

Beyond the style and the imagery, however, the reader is
fascinated by the author's ability to deal effectively with the
greatest and most universal subjects: be it death, human nature,
beauty, Chateaubriand is a master of his subject. As with all
truly classic authors, in the most basic sense of that term, he
instinctively seeks out and deals with the most fundamental
and most general concerns of mankind. He may do it, in the
manner of the Romantics, by presenting his subject in the most
individualized manifestation possible, but the universal attraction
of his subject is amply documented by his continued, and frequently impassioned readership.

Notes and References

Chapter One

1. He was baptized François René. He always seems to refer to himself as François-Auguste, however. Was this ignorance, or did he reserve René for his "secret" name, his literary other self?

2. To avoid confusion, the *Memoirs* will be referred to by book and chapter. These indications remain constant throughout the various editions in which the work appeared.

3. Louis XVI and his family left the palace in the middle of the night, intending to flee the country. Near the northeastern frontier, the king was recognized, arrested, and returned to Paris. Legend has it that someone recognized the king from his portrait on a gold piece (the undeniable Bourbon nose would make this seem logical), but the flight was so amateurishly organized that any number of elements could have provoked discovery.

4. Son of the prince de Condé and one of the royalist leaders.

5. Book 23 of the *Memoirs* deals with Napoleon's *Hundred Days*.

Chapter Two

1. References to the *Genius* will be to part, book, and chapter.

2. The problems raised by this American setting will be discussed in Chapter 5, "Chateaubriand's America."

3. The question of style will be examined in Chapter 10.

4. The Abbé Prévost published his short novel, *Manon Lescaut,* in 1731. It was rapidly recognized as one of the true classics of the novel form. Some critics suggest it was out of ignorance that Prévost described the area around New Orleans, where the end of the story is placed, as a sandy desert. However, his interest in travel books (he edited and published a series of them) would not seem to support this theory.

5. See Richard Switzer, *Chateaubriand Today* (Madison, Wis., 1970), pp. 153 ff.

6. The Abencerrajes were a well-known Moorish line. Chateaubriand uses a gallicized form of the name in the original title: Abencérages.

7. The most recent pronouncement reaffirms the denial that Chateaubriand and Natalie de Noailles did in fact meet in the Alhambra (see item 231 of the Bibliothèque Nationale catalogue of the

Chateaubriand Bicentenary Exposition of 1969: *Chateaubriand, le voyageur et l'homme politique.*

Chapter Three

1. See the passage from II, ii, 1, quoted in Chapter 2 (p. 43).

2. "Like long echos which melt into one another from afar . . . perfumes, colors and sounds evoke one another." Baudelaire first published his collection of poems, *The Flowers of Evil,* in 1857.

3. References are to Chateaubriand's divisions of parts, books, and chapters, rather than to any specific editions.

4. The Syrian ruins of Palmyra, which had only recently been discovered by the Europeans, were particularly famous at this time.

Chapter Four

1. It must be admitted, however, that frequently his memory betrayed him, and the quotations were not quite accurate. This is interesting in itself, however, since it proves the quotation was from memory, not from the printed text.

2. Molière, in his plays, frequently uses the novel as the point of his satire.

3. V. L. Tapié, *Chateaubriand par lui-même* (Paris, 1965), p. 89.

4. Preface to the first edition.

5. Book V. The situation is similar to that recounted by Voltaire in *The Ingenuous One,* and even the language is similar.

Chapter Five

1. From a review of J. P. Richard's *Paysage de Chateaubriand* in the [London] *Times Literary Supplement,* LXVI (Dec. 14, 1967), p. 1216.

2. See these passages quoted in Chapter 3.

3. *Travels in America* (Lexington, Kentucky, 1969), pp. 11-12.

4. This and other portions of the abbé de Mondésir's diary were published by Victor Giraud together with his edition of *Atala.*

5. *Oeuvres complètes* (Garnier), I, p. 363.

6. *Ibid.,* V, pp. 422-23.

Chapter Six

1. The following are the principal works falling into this category:
   Essay on Revolutions (1797)
   On Buonaparte and the Bourbons (1814)
   Political Reflections (1814)

On Monarchy According to the Charter (1816)
The King Is Dead, Long Live the King (1824)
On the Reestablishment of Censorship (1827)
On the Restoration and Elective Monarchy (1831)
On the Banishment of Charles X and His Family (1831)
On the Captivity of the Duchess de Berry (1832)
The Congress of Verona (1838)

In addition, the articles from the newspapers and journals have been collected and reproduced in many editions of the *Complete Works*.

2. Some justification may be needed here. The writings on Spanish America have certainly not been among his best-known political works. However, the other political works have to a great extent lost their interest, dealing with abstractions and situations no longer relevant. The opposite is true of the Spanish American writings.

3. *Oeuvres complètes* (Garnier), XII, 34.

4. *Ibid.*, p. 342.

5. English translation: University of Kentucky Press, 1969.

6. In the *Oeuvres complètes* (Garnier), VII.

7. *Ibid.*, XII.

8. *Ibid.*

9. *Ibid.*

10. Chateaubriand suggests this in *ibid.*, p. 45.

11. *Ibid.*, p. 80.

12. *Ibid.*, p. 35.

13. Reports from the British ambassador in Paris show that this idea was indeed a constant preoccupation of Chateaubriand.

14. *Ibid.*, p. 51.

15. *Ibid.*, p. 46. The official designations of the monarchs are: Catholic Majesty, Spain; Most Christian Majesty, France; Britannic Majesty, Great Britain. The quotation is from Chateaubriand's speech at the congress. In his written text he adds this clarification: "Here can be seen the germination of the idea of this general congress, by means of which we wished to terminate one day the Spanish War, if that war was to take place, in order to pacify the world by the creation of new, constitutional Bourbon monarchies in America."

16. *Ibid.*, p. 49.

17. *Ibid.*

18. "Negociations," *Ibid.*, p. 342. We must again note Chateaubriand's peculiar ability to rejoice in the triumph of an undesirable individual, if he finds the cause a just one.

19. *Ibid.*, VIII, 283.

20. *Ibid.*, XII, 364.

21. *Travels in America*, p. 191.

22. *Ibid.*, pp. 192-93.

Chapter Seven

1. Traditional criticism has seen a reversal in Chateaubriand's attitudes: pro-*philosophe* in the *Essay*, anti-*philosophe* afterward. The break, however, is not as abrupt as it might at first seem. See Robert Shackleton's article in *Chateaubriand Today*.

2. Charles Florisoone and V. L. Tapié, *Chateaubriand* (Paris: Hatier, 1948), p. 407.

3. The Eighteenth century had seen the breakdown of the classical rules of the theater: no mixture of tragic and comic, presentation of only noble characters in the tragedy, and the like. The "discovery" of Shakespeare by the French authors did much to hasten the development of a new esthetic. Victor Hugo's manifesto of the new theatre, the preface to his play *Cromwell*, had appeared ten years before Chateaubriand's *Essay on English Literature*.

4. *Essay on English Literature*, Part II.

Chapter Eight

1. At least four editions are currently available: Garnier-Flammarion, 10/18, Club français du livre, Bibliothèque d'aujourd'hui.

2. Gracq's pun is untranslatable. The French word for "scribble" is *griffonner*, which suggests the mythical griffon.

3. Julien Gracq, *Un beau ténébreux* (Paris: Club français du livre, n.d.), pp. 148-49.

4. *Vie de Rancé* (Paris: Jean Valmont, n.d.), p. 10.

Chapter Nine

1. This is a famous painting by Baron François Gérard (1790-1837) of Mme de Staël posed as the heroine of her then-famous novel *Corinne*. She is seated, dressed in flowing robes, holding a lyre at her feet. The French post office used this painting as the subject of a postage stamp issued in 1960 in honor of Mme de Staël.

2. i.e., Mme Récamier.

3. Pourrat edition of the complete works, I, 39-40.

4. More or less concurrently with the Centenary edition, Levaillant was preparing the Pléiade edition, the first volume of which appeared in 1946.

5. The poem Chateaubriand quotes is Parny's "Le Raccommodement" from his collection *Poésies érotiques*, II.

Selected Bibliography

PRIMARY SOURCES

1. Important editions of complete or collected works:
   Oeuvres complètes. Paris: Ladvocat, 1826-31. 28 volumes. First edition of the complete works, including the first editions of several important texts.
   Oeuvres complètes. Paris: Pourrat, 1836-39. 36 volumes. Augmented edition, including particularly the important introductory biographical essay.
   Oeuvres complètes. Paris: Garnier, n.d. 12 volumes. The most easily available edition, kept in print for almost a hundred years. Volume 12 includes an index to the complete works.
   Oeuvres romanesques et voyages. Paris: Bibliothèque de la Pléiade, 1969. 2 volumes. Contains all the principal fiction and travels.
2. Import editions of the *Memoirs* (not included in any of the *Complete Works*):
   Mémoires d'Outre-Tombe. Paris: Flammarion, 1948. 4 volumes.
   Mémoires d'Outre-Tombe. Paris: Bibliothèque de la Pléiade, 1946. 2 volumes.
3. Presently available French texts of individual works:
   Atala, René, Les Aventures du dernier Abencérage. Paris: Garnier, 1958.
   Génie du christianisme. Paris: Garnier-Flammarion, 1966. 2 volumes.
   Itinéraire de Paris à Jérusalem. Paris: Julliard, 1964.
   Politique de Chateaubriand. Paris: Armand Colin, 1967. An anthology of Chateaubriand's political writings.
   Vie de Rancé. Paris: 10-18, 1965.
   Voyage en Amérique. Paris: Didier, 1964. 2 volumes.
4. Currently available texts in English translation:
   Atala and René. Berkeley: University of California, 1952.
   Memoirs. London and New York, 1961. Selections.
   Travels in America. Lexington: University of Kentucky Press, 1969.

SECONDARY SOURCES

BASSAN, FERNANDE. *Chateaubriand et la Terre-Sainte.* Paris: Presses Universitaries de France, 1959. A thorough examination of the travels from Paris to Jerusalem.

CHINARD, GILBERT. *L'Exotisme américain dans l'oeuvre de Chateaubriand.* Paris: Hachette, 1918. Still the outstanding work in the area of exoticism.

CHRISTOPHOROV, PIERRE. *Sur les pas de Chateaubriand en exil.* Paris: Ed. de Minuit, 1961. A new examination of the English years with much new material.

DURRY, MARIE-JEANNE. *La Vieillesse de Chateaubriand.* Paris: Le Divan, 1933. 2 volumes. An outstanding interpretation of the later years.

EVANS, JOAN. *Chateaubriand.* London: Macmillan, 1939. Excellent, somewhat romanticized portrait, by a highly competent biographer.

FLORISSONE, CHARLES, and V. L. TAPIÉ. *Chateaubriand.* Paris: Hatier, 1948. Extracts from the works with introductions and notes. Excellent for giving over-all sense of the various works.

GRACQ, JULIEN. "Réflexions sur Chateaubriand." *Cahiers du Sud,* L (1960), 163-72. An incisive appraisal by one of the great modern novelists; one of the essential documents in the critical re-evaluation of Chateaubriand in modern times.

LE BRAZ, ANATOLE. *Au Pays d'exil de Chateaubriand.* Paris: Champion, 1909. An early but still good study of Chateaubriand's years of exile; by one of the better-known regionalist novelists.

LEVAILLANT, MAURICE. *Chateaubriand, Madame Récamier et les Mémoires d'Outre-Tombe.* 3rd edition. Paris: Delagrave, 1947. Authoritative study of Chateaubriand's masterpiece and the circumstances of composition, by one of the most eminent of Chateaubriand scholars.

————. *Chateaubriand, Prince des songes.* Paris: Hachette, 1960. A fine interpretation and appreciation of Chateaubriand's poetic qualities.

————. *Splendeurs et misères de M. de Chateaubriand.* 6th edition. Paris: Albin Michel, 1948. Reedition of an old (1922) but still basic work in Chateaubriand criticism.

MARTIN-CHAUFFIER, LOUIS. *Chateaubriand.* Paris, 1969. Good basic introduction to Chateaubriand. Excellent iconographical material. One of a well-received literary series ("Ecrivains d'hier et d'aujourd'hui").

MAUROIS, ANDRÉ. *Chateaubriand.* Paris: Grasset, 1938. A good general biography by one of the most popular biographers. Available in English translation (New York and London: Harper, 1938).

MOREAU, PIERRE. *Chateaubriand.* Paris: Desclée, 1965. Thorough study of Chateaubriand, especially from the spiritual point of view.

————. *Chateaubriand, l'homme et l'oeuvre.* Paris: Hatier, 1956. Excellent basic study in a well-established series.

RICHARD, JEAN-PIERRE. *Paysage de Chateaubriand.* Paris: Seuil, 1967. The outstanding example of "new criticism" of Chateaubriand.

SAINTE-BEUVE, C. A. *Chateaubriand et son groupe littéraire sous l'Empire.* Paris: Garnier, 1949. Very partial in its assessments, but still a classic work of criticism by one of the great critics. This was a course taught by Sainte-Beuve at Liège in 1848-49.

SWITZER, RICHARD. *Chateaubriand Today.* Madison: University of Wisconsin Press, 1970. A collection of studies in French and English centering on the lasting values of Chateaubriand's work.

TAPIÉ, VICTOR-L. *Chateaubriand par lui-même.* Paris: Seuil, 1965. Fine basic introductory study, with excellent illustrative materials.

WALKER, THOMAS C. *Chateaubriand's Natural Scenery.* Baltimore: Johns Hopkins, 1946. A carefule examination of Chateaubriand's descriptive art.

Index

169